WHY DO FOOLS...?

Understanding Human Sexual Strategies

Steven Hedlesky, MD, FACEP

ISBN: 0615761720

ISBN 13: 9780615761725

Library of Congress Control Number: 2013902983
CreateSpace Independent Publishing Platform,
North Charleston, SC

Acknowledgements

It is certainly true that no book is written by one person. A great many people were involved in this work. I especially want to thank Jovana for having suggested that I write down all my ideas. Jessica, Jon, Grace, Ashley, Shannon, Jim, Allison, Lindsey, and many others gave me encouragement and valuable information.

Over the decades that I have worked in the ER, hundreds of individuals have shared with me the details of their personal lives. I want to acknowledge their courage and tell them that they are all OK. Most of them were worried at the time that they were somehow abnormal, but they all fit in. They all have legitimate places in human society.

I also want to thank the unsung heroes of the publishing industry, those friends, co-workers, and relatives, including my mother, who reviewed the early drafts, painful as it might have been. They were universally supportive and positive. I am fortunate to have them and they deserve a share of the credit for this publication.

Table of Contents

Introduction

We sleep in separate rooms, we have dinner apart, and we take separate vacations. We're doing everything we can to keep our marriage together.

RODNEY DANGERFIELD

Professional comedians know that nothing can be funny unless it contains a true premise. Will Rogers said, "I have always noticed that people will never laugh at anything that is not based on truth." We can all identify with Rodney's remark, because we recognize his sentiment. We know that human beings do not easily live together as couples. After a few years, they settle into a state of chronic conflict.

I have done that twice, through two marriages, each lasting more than a decade before ending in divorce. And so I asked myself the following two questions: If humans are meant to live together as lifelong couples, then why is monogamy so hard to do? On the other hand, if they are not meant to be monogamous, then why do they try so hard to pretend that they are?

I have worked as an Emergency Room physician on the night shift, observing humanity, for the past twenty-five years. Like an urban anthropologist, I see modern humans at their most primitive moments, in their natural state. In the early hours of the morning, people will reveal the most intimate details of their lives. I have accumulated a quarter of a century of observations about relationships and social conflict. I will share some of them here. The people I will introduce you to in these pages are not urban social adventurers.

They are small-town, everyday people with routine lives. But they are each special in surprising ways that reveal the true nature of human relationships.

I am one of those people. This book began as a series of essays that I wrote to try to understand the turmoil in my second marriage. It has become part of my healing process, and it can help heal others. There is nothing unique in my experience. In each of my marriages, my spouse and I tried to do everything right. We provided well for our family, cared for our children, performed our marital duties, and respected our vows. But still, my first marriage fell apart after twenty-three years, and then a second marriage crumbled after only eleven years. I could not understand why.

Ultimately I approached this problem in the same way that I would handle any stubborn clinical problem in my practice. I researched the current literature, read the most respected books on the subject, reviewed the old literature, looked over my own experiences and the cases in my own practice, and tried to come to an understanding of human loving.

Now, after four decades of marriage, three decades of observations in the ER, twenty-six years of raising children, and an extensive review of the literature, I understand that we humans do not work the way we have been told. The traditional models of romance are more than just flawed. They are simply wrong. The love that is portrayed in storybooks, music, and movies bears no resemblance to real human mating behavior. The "True Love" of *The Princess Bride* and the "Happily Ever After" of *Cinderella* are no more real than Santa Clause.

So I challenge you to discard all your previous notions and follow along with me as we discover how human relationships really work. Starting with a few basic biological principles, we will explore why we act the way we do toward one another based on one simple premise: We are biologically primitive creatures in a technologically modern world, and our genetically programmed instincts are in conflict with the demands of contemporary society and culture.

We really are primitive creatures. Modern humans appeared during the Middle Stone Age, which ended about 10,000 years ago. They were tool-using primates living in small groups, sexually promiscuous, with no awareness of the connection between sex and children, and no concept of paternity. The last Stone Age ended about 5000 years ago when humans domesticated horses and cattle and invented the wheel. They developed plow based agriculture and metallurgy and created the concepts of property and inheritance. And, as we shall see, they robbed women of most of their human rights. The world of today bears little resemblance to the world we came from. The entire transition from the Middle Stone Age to modern Western industrial culture, from flint-knapping hunter-gatherers to young urban professionals, occurred in a mere 10,000 years.

Ten millennia is too little time for changes to occur in the genetic programming of basic mating behavior. Despite the advances of civilization, we humans have the same genes and the same mating instincts that we had in the Stone Ages. Our culture and lifestyle have changed tremendously, but we, as a species, have not. Our modern civilized rules of behavior are not compatible with the instincts programmed into our genes. As a result, we are expected to behave in ways that just do not feel right to us. This is one of the two main sources of the conflict in our interpersonal relationships.

The other source is the pure competition between us as individuals. We are each programmed to propagate our own genes, to give our own progeny the best chance to populate the planet for the future. You, dear reader, are the product of a long line of ancestors who managed to find and retain mates, breed with them, and raise children to adulthood. They did so against astounding odds, out-competing their adversaries and surviving the hazards of their environments for thousands upon thousands of generations. You have inherited the genes of millions of winners, and, whether you know it or not, you are a savagely competitive creature. Your DNA compels you to compete. Like all humans, you are genetically programmed to cooperate with others, including your own spouse, only when it benefits your own children. This book explains why we humans compete not only against our adversaries, but also against our spouses. It explores how we can learn to live at peace with our partners and with our own human nature.

As we go along, we will discover answers to some of the more intriguing questions about human relationships, such as: Why do people fall in love, and fall out of love? Why do so many marriages end in divorce? Why do so many couples become good friends again after they divorce? What is the purpose of the human female orgasm? Why are human babies so helpless and difficult to care for? Why do men, and women, sometimes do such foolish things? Why do people stay in bad relationships? How do people in some cultures tolerate arranged marriages? Why do good girls like bad boys? Why are some people homosexual, or bisexual? How do the genes for homosexuality stay in the population? Do homosexuals reproduce, and, if so, how? Why have men historically had such dominance over women? How did the division of labor in childrearing turn into such a lopsided distribution of privileges between the sexes? And why is it so hard to correct this inequality? The answers to many of these questions are not at all intuitive in the framework of modern cultures, but become obvious when the subject is viewed from the correct perspective.

Humor is a powerful teaching tool, not only because it keeps the reader's interest, but also because jokes are a special window into the workings of the mind. A joke cannot be funny unless it is based on a plausible premise, but by being plausible, a joke reveals an underlying truth. Often, it is the conflict between different truths, or the incongruity between different versions of reality that is interpreted as being funny. Laughter is a way for humans to dissipate the stress that arises from that conflict. Consider the following simple joke, adapted from a Zits comic strip.

Boy says to girl, "Do you like Guinea pigs."
She responds, "Oh! I love Guinea pigs."
He says, "Wonderful. So do I. Let's get together and compare recipes."

The sudden, unexpected reversal of the boy's intentions creates a conflict that some people will interpret as pathos or cruelty and others will find funny. This sort of humor illustrates the relationship between comedy and tragedy that often confuses beginning students of literature. Humor is a mechanism that humans use to deal with cognitive conflict or incongruity. It is a stress dissipation device.

This joke reveals a profound truth. The word *love* can mean many different things, and not all of them are beneficial to the object of that love. The girl uses *love* to mean affection, while the boy uses it to talk about food. The conflict between the two opposite meanings of *love* is interpreted as humorous.

The joke only works because the two opposing realities exist. On the one hand, people adore Guinea pigs and keep them as pets. On the other hand, people can eat Guinea pigs, and still do in some places in the world. The sudden intrusion of the latter reality upon the girl and her pet is interpreted as humorous. The joke simply would not work if non-edible objects like hand tools or Ming Dynasty vases were substituted for the Guinea pigs. The premise has to be plausible in order for the joke to be funny. Many sources of information about relationships can deceive, but jokes are constrained to the truth. Off-color jokes provide a delightfully honest insight into the workings of human reproductive relationships.

Throughout the book, I have purposely avoided the controversy between evolution and creationism. I am writing about the mechanics of human behavior, and not about the origins of humans. Regardless of how we came to be here, we can all agree that some similarities exist between modern humans, ancient humans, and certain animals. Perhaps this is because we all have the same problems to solve on a day-today basis: finding food, seeking shelter, avoiding predators, finding mates, and reproducing.

Maybe we were built by a creator, using some of the same sub-systems as lower animals, but with added features that are unique to humans. Or maybe we humans evolved from lower animals. I use these concepts interchangeably, sometimes referring to how humans evolved, and other times discussing their design. I am not investigating how we came to be here. I am interested only in what we are and how our reproductive relationships function.

The material in this book naturally divides into three sections. Chapters one through eight deal with the emotional bonds that occur between two people when they form a pair. For simplicity of language, I have focused on heterosexual couples, but everything in these chapters applies equally well to same-sex relationships. I argue against the notion of humans as monogamous creatures, and, instead, adopt the concept of pair-bonding. In humans, this is a temporary bond lasting four to seven years. It begins with the process known as falling in love, and ends with the inevitable process of falling out of love. I follow with a discussion of the emotional components and social mechanics of romantic, post-romantic, and non-romantic relationships.

Chapters nine through twelve deal with the social aspects of reproductive pairing. Marriage is reviewed from the earliest primate proto-romance through human pre-history and continuing through the Mesolithic, Neolithic, and modern ages. The politics of paternity are a crucial part of this history and a large part of this section is dedicated to the conflict between men and women regarding the control of paternity. In particular, I include a section dedicated to the female orgasm and its role in paternity, society, politics, religion, and war.

Chapters thirteen through sixteen are about sexual preference and diversity. Human sexuality can be analyzed with a mathematical model. Homosexuality and bisexuality can be explained in terms of population statistics. Human behaviors are spread out over standard distribution curves, and some people fall, by chance, in overlapping areas between the two sexes. This creates the diversity and versatility that are part of the normal spectrum of human sexuality. Similar sexual diversity exists elsewhere in the animal kingdom: there is no logical basis for labeling homosexuality as un-natural. As with any other characteristic of a population, sexual diversity exists because it provides some reproductive advantage.

I hope that this book will help readers understand their own behaviors and emotions better. We can all learn to deal more effectively with the conflicts that we feel when our primitive instincts collide with the norms of contemporary cultures. A more realistic understanding of our emotional bonds will help alleviate the feelings of shame, guilt, and resentment that arise as relationships mature, and that so often lead to the abandonment of those relationships.

I also hope this book will convince readers that homosexual and bisexual pairings are no different than heterosexual pairing, and that all forms of loving have their own legitimate roles in the continuation of the human species. This will lead to a better understanding and appreciation of the sexual diversity and versatility with which we humans are so endowed.

1

Basic Human Mating Behavior

There is no fundamental difference in the ways of thinking of
primitive and civilized man.

FRANZ BOAS

Thoughts on Behalf of a Young Woman

Caroline is a junior colleague of mine. When I met her, she
was twenty-eight, a professional, a wife, and a mother of one
child. She was very bright, pretty, and well educated, and
yet she struggled with some basic biological decisions. After
five years of marriage, she had separated from her husband,
in what she anticipated would be a temporary arrangement.
Only four months later, she found herself falling in love with

another man. Having been raised as a Catholic, she struggled to reconcile her emotions with her religious beliefs. When Caroline brought all this to my attention, we were both at work in the ER, and we were extremely hurried. I had to condense my advice into the following very short historical synopsis.

The Muslim laws of marriage, recorded about 700 C.E, were written by men. The Judeo-Christian laws of marriage, recorded in the Old Testament 2000 years ago, were also written by men. The earliest known written laws of marriage, recorded in the Hammurabi Code 3,700 years, were written by men. Yet, the genetic code that runs Caroline's body and controls her emotions was created millions of years ago, and was written by God. I told Caroline to ask herself why she would allow men to overrule what God tells her body to do.

Caroline is afflicted with a dilemma that is ubiquitous in modern humans. I asked her a *why* question, and part of the answer is that she is doing what she has been taught to do. However, she has been taught to behave in a way that does not feel right to her. Each of us has a program written in our genetic code that tells us what feels right and what feels wrong, and Caroline has been told that what feels right to her is wrong. She has been taught to behave in a manner that contradicts her genetic programming. Human behaviors are directed by genetic code. Our bodies and minds follow the instructions recorded in our DNA. As we humans became civilized, we learned to deviate from some of those behaviors for the sake of civility, but we have deviated so far that we have lost awareness of the source of our emotions. As a result, we have become burdened with guilt and shame for having what are essentially normal emotions. A great deal of personal suffering and strife could be avoided if we had a better understanding of our bodies and of the primitive parts of our brains.

Why

The question *Why?* is ambiguous. If you ask why people engage in a particular behavior, you are asking six different questions.

1. How did an individual acquire the behavior? Was it hardwired into her genes? Was it taught to her by her mother?

2. Why does the behavior persist in the person? What reward does she receive from it?

3. How does this behavior improve this person's survival such that she passes this behavior on to her progeny?

4. How did this behavior get introduced to the person's community. Was it invented? Was it a new mutation? Was it imported from another culture?

5. Why does the behavior persist in the community? What is the incentive for practice of the behavior?

6. How does this behavior benefit the reproductive success of the population, such that this culture competes successfully against other cultures?

Consider two behaviors: wearing shoes and smoking tobacco.

For the first, the answers are: 1. Taught by mother. 2. Less pain in feet. 3. Fewer foot injuries and infections. 4. Invented or imported. 5. Increased community health. 6. Increased military success.

For the second behavior, smoking tobacco: 1. Taught by peers. 2. Feels good and reduces anxiety. 3. Unknown. 4. Introduced from another culture. 5. Provided a tax base to the American colonies. 6. Profitable export to other cultures.

As this book progresses, the question *why* will be directed toward many different sexual behaviors, including *Falling in Love*.

Reproductive Basics

Somewhere inside every human being there is a biological organism with the need to propagate its genes. Humans have to reproduce, for the simple reason that they do not live forever. They have to make replacements for themselves. Those who did not make replacements are no longer around.

The part of you that is in charge of your reproductive instincts is in the brainstem, the most primitive part of the brain. Deep within you, underneath the religion, education, and socialization, there is a part of you that is merely a vehicle designed to carry your genetic material forward in time to the next generation. Every organism alive today is genetically programmed to perform that function, because those who could not do so have all died out. This underlying organism deep within you, and separate from your persona, controls your basic breeding instincts.

Reproductive instincts are uniform throughout a species. That is the definition of a species. The members must be able to breed and create fertile offspring. Two animals with incompatible breeding instincts cannot reproduce. Details as insignificant as single notes in a mating call or the hues of pebbles in a nest can exclude birds from mating. Mating instincts must be absolutely compatible between members of a species. Human dating and marriage customs may vary between cultures and religions, but breeding instincts do not. In all cultures, men and women have the same set of primitive needs and desires because they are all of the same species. All humans respond to the same cues.

Those cues are programmed in our genes. Genes control reproductive instincts. In his book, *The Selfish Gene*, Richard Dawkins demonstrates that, in a biologically competitive world, genes propagate themselves at the expense of other genes.

They have no morals, chivalry, altruism, or empathy. They are relatively simple fragments of DNA, the chemical that carries the genetic code. Genes are self-propagating mechanical pieces of information. They have no more ethics than a virus. They exist far below the outer shell of personality and culture, deep within the nucleus of every cell. Genes set the ground rules for reproductive behavior. They determine breeding instincts. The number-one instinct is selfishness, simply because those genes that were not selfish have vanished from the population.

The primary role of genes is to propagate themselves, but they do so by propagating their hosts. All genes that have survived into the present have done so by succeeding at this task. Every behavior that genes tell the body to do is directed toward reproducing those genes. Reproduction is the principle function of all living creatures, at least among those species that still exist, and it is the primary function for which humans are designed. Admittedly, many humans no longer choose to reproduce. In the contemporary world, people have other reasons to live, now that their survival as a species is assured. But this is a social change, not a change in human nature. Instinctive behaviors were shaped by the absolute need to reproduce, and they have not changed in the past ten millennia. Reproduction is the motivation that shapes human behavior.

None of our basic instincts about breeding require any understanding of the link between sex and babies. Primitive humans did not make that connection. They did not have sex in order to have children. They had sex in order to form alliances, obtain favors, make friends, and receive and give pleasure. Babies were an unforeseen byproduct. Humans are designed to want sex under certain conditions and with certain types of people, but it is not because they reason out the best strategy for survival. People with those desires simply had more children, grandchildren, and great grandchildren, so now all the humans alive today have those behaviors.

Neither a man nor a woman can reproduce alone. This concept may seem obvious, but it has important implications. In order for a man to propagate his genes, he must also propagate those of a woman. Likewise, in order for a woman to propagate her genes, she must also propagate those of a man. But the two sexes have widely divergent roles in the reproductive process. Their concerns when selecting mates are very different, and this is where human reproductive behavior gets complicated.

In humans, as in all mammals, the female makes a limited number of eggs in her lifetime. She can produce only a small number of children, each of which requires a large investment on her part. She has the womb and the breasts. She is the one who bears the greatest share of the burden in nourishing and raising a baby. She cannot just walk away from a pregnancy. She is stuck with her choices. It is in her best interest to be highly selective in her choice of a male to fertilize her ova.

The human female is relatively immobilized by the burden of small children. The large human brain necessitates a large head, which complicates the birthing process, especially in an animal that stands on her hind legs and walks upright. A woman must have a wide birth canal to allow the passage of a human baby's head, and this requires a wide pelvis. But a wide pelvis causes problems. If the pelvis is too wide, the angle formed by the thighbone and the leg bone at the knee becomes too great, and causes the kneecap to pop out of place. So, a human female also needs a narrow pelvis in order to stand upright.

The solution to this engineering dilemma is to birth the baby before the head becomes too large, but that means the baby will be born while still very immature. Human infants require a great deal more care than other newborn mammals. Most infant mammals can walk when only a few days old. Some can walk within minutes of their birth. It will be two years before a human child can reliably walk unassisted.

The infant's dependency means there must be a division of labor in the human family. Under natural conditions, the human mother must carry and feed her child for the first two years. The burden of caring for the child limits the mother's ability to provide for herself and the child. She will be at a disadvantage when competing with other humans for food and resources. She will not be able to range over long distances quickly, or to escape predators. Her hands will be occupied by children and will not be free to gather food, brandish weapons, or use tools. The human mother and her small child will have a greater chance of survival if she has assistance. The female who can keep a mate at her side, helping and protecting her and the child, will be at a definite advantage over females who cannot. More of her children will survive to become healthy progeny. Note that her mate does not need to be the father of the child and does not even need to be a male.

Males do not have such restrictions. Unburdened by the need to feed an infant at frequent intervals, the male can range over a wide territory to hunt for food. With both hands free, he can carry resources long distances. With greater muscle mass, he is able to provide shelter from the elements and protection from animals and from other humans.

The reproductive role of the human male is very different from that of the female. Male mammals produce an almost unlimited number of sperm. A man can have a huge number of children, limited only by the number of women he can access. To propagate his genes, a man needs only to copulate with any woman. Just as he is free to hunt game and resources, he is also free to roam in search of other females. He does not need to be concerned with the rearing of children that result from chance liaisons with women other than his mate. He is not obligated to raise those children. He can simply leave them to be raised by their mothers.

Of course, a man's offspring will have a better chance of survival if the mother has the support and protection of a mate. But there is no biological reason that the mate supporting her must be the man who fathered her children. A gallivanting male can impregnate a woman and leave her in the care of another man. He begets additional offspring at no cost to himself. The flip side of the coin is that an enterprising woman can choose a man other than her mate to father her children. She may obtain a better selection of genetic material (a more attractive biological father) for her offspring, and still retain the support of her mate. She may also obtain additional resources for her child from her opportunistic sex partner.

This introduces one of the two main sources of all the conflict between men and women. Each of us is programmed with the drive to maximize the propagation of our own genes at the expense of all others. Each of us does so by offering what we have in exchange for what the opposite sex needs. Men have resources, and men want opportunities to copulate with women. Women have the ability to produce babies, and women need resources for their support and that of their children. They also need the most attractive sex partner they can find. Each sex is looking for the most return on their investment. Each of them is instinctively driven to obtain the best possible deal for their own genes, even if it means betraying their own partner.

Human Mating Strategies

The division of labor in human childrearing and the separate short-term and long-term mating strategies for males and females can place the male and female in adversarial positions. Both males and females strive to form reproductive pairs, working together to raise their young. But they both also have instincts that push them to stray from their mates. Females are genetically programmed to seek out opportunities for sex with males who are more attractive, have more political power, or possess greater wealth than their mates. Males are programmed to seek extra-pair couplings, but with any available females, without regard for the resultant offspring.

This is why human relationships are so variable in quality and character. Relationships can range all the way from purely symbiotic, as when two parents faithfully work together to raise their shared offspring, to purely predatory or parasitic, as when women are impregnated through rape, or men are deceived about the paternity of children. Men and women are genetically equipped to cooperate with each other, but they also have the ability to take advantage of each other. Genes are selfish. Genes are designed to reproduce themselves at the expense of all others. Reproduction is a highly competitive and dangerous game, and when people have sex, some of them get screwed.

The Lady in the Bar

A man walks into a bar and sees a pretty woman sitting by herself on a barstool.
He walks up to her and says, "Hi. How's it going?"
She turns to him, looks deep into his eyes, and says, "I'll screw anybody, anytime, anywhere, for any reason. My place, your place, anywhere you like, it doesn't matter."
He says, "No kidding! So what law firm are you with?"

Anonymous

This is a very intriguing joke. It is based on a homonym. Homonyms are pairs of words that have different meanings, but are pronounced and spelled the same. They often have some common root in their etymologies.

For example, consider the word *bank*, as in a riverbank, and also as in a financial institution. These two uses of the word have the same root meaning. A bank was once a pile of stored resources, such as coal, firewood, or grain. The use of the word later diverged to mean a place where resources are kept for later use (financial institution), and also a sloping physical feature resembling a pile of material (river bank). Homonyms reveal hidden relationships in the workings of human culture.

The "Lady in the bar" exploits the conflict that occurs between two people who become lovers. The word *screw* is a homonym, with several different meanings, all with some consanguinity. It is a slang word meaning to copulate or engage in sex. In a mechanical sense, the word means to force an object into an opening by twisting or turning, and the relationship to copulation is obvious. However, *screw* also has the following synonyms: cheat, defraud, deceive, victimize, betray, and take advantage of. What do these have to do with making love?

When two people become lovers, they often each have their own hidden agendas, their own private purposes, for the interaction. These agendas may or may not be harmful to the other party. So, when lovers commit themselves to a sexual act, they place themselves at considerable risk, in terms of disease, reputation, financial obligations, pregnancy, physical injury, and personal conflict. Both parties in a sexual relationship put their social capital at risk, and both are vulnerable, naked, and exposed, to use other words that are common to both the bedroom and the courtroom.

The human female is genetically programmed to obtain as many resources as she can for her offspring, even if these are obtained from males who are not related to her offspring. This is why she continues to be sexually active when she is not fertile or when she is already pregnant. She knows instinctively that males will offer her incentives, in the form of resources, in return for opportunities to mate with her, even when their efforts do not benefit their genes.

The human male is genetically programmed to attach himself to a female and support her and his offspring at least for the time required to raise those offspring through weaning. It benefits a man to invest resources in the mother of his children. They will be more likely to survive to reproductive age, and his genes will be more likely to persist in the gene pool.

However, the human male is also programmed to mate with as many other females as possible, with as little expenditure of resources as possible. His instinct is to mate with any available female, especially if someone else ends up supporting the offspring. Men are inclined to provide resources to any female who offers them the promise of sex. But men also try to minimize their investments in these other females. That is, they try to get sex for as little as possible.

An old adage teaches that men court women in order to obtain sex, while women promise sex in order to get courtship. In human relationships, men need sex, and women need gifts. Men need affection, and women need commitment. Men use the promise of commitment to obtain sex, while women advertise their sexuality in order to obtain resources. It is all just biological. Are they using each other? Well, yes, but that is what they are designed to do.

The lesson

A young lady comes home from school one day and tells her mother that today she learned how mommies get babies. Her mother was a little surprised but listened as the girl explained what her friend, Julie, had told her during school.

Julie told how she had peeked into her parents' bedroom and seen her mother and father naked on the bed. The mother kissed her father's "thing", and put it in her mouth over and over again until he shook all over.

"Oh no," said the girl's mother, "that's not how mommies get babies. That's how mommies get jewelry."

This is one out of hundreds of jokes that exploit this particular aspect of human sexuality.

Here we come to the heart of the matter. If we ask the simple question, "Why do people have sex?" we get the naïve answer, "Because it feels good." But, if we ask the specific question, "What is the primary function of sexual behavior in humans?" we get different answers for the male and the female. For a human male, the primary function of sex is to impregnate the female and beget offspring. For a female, the primary function of sex is to obtain resources from males for the support of herself and her children.

Under primitive conditions, the most biologically successful woman will be the one who has the most men helping to support herself and her children, especially if some of those men are not the fathers of her children. On the other hand, the most biologically successful man is the one who can impregnate the most women, especially if other men provide support for those women and his children.

The barter system that worked well for primitive people in the past, and still does in some parts of the world, has been replaced in the modern world by well regulated mating behaviors entrenched in etiquette, law, religion, and society. Today the rules of civility dictate appropriate reproductive behavior. But civilization is only a thin veneer. We are still primitive creatures.

That is the other reason that there is so much conflict in modern human relationships. We are taught by our elders to believe in certain ideals of romance. But our instincts compel us to behave in an entirely different manner. This is precisely where my junior colleague Caroline finds herself. She is torn between obeying the lessons of her upbringing and answering the call of her own genetic programming. To use a computer analogy, her modern software is not compatible with her prehistoric operating system.

Humans fall in love again quickly when they find themselves alone. In times of personal crisis, natural disaster, or war, the ancient behaviors quickly re-emerge. People revert to their basic instincts. This was well documented in the aftermath of World War II. German cities were occupied by American soldiers who had money, food, and other resources to spare. Those cities were filled with local women, many with children, who were either widowed, or in uncertain status. The German women readily cohabitated with American GIs, the men who may have killed their husbands, in order to obtain the resources they needed for themselves and their children.

The most faithful wife feels compelled to turn to an alternative man when her children are hungry and her husband's fate is unknown. She will obtain food and protection from any available man, and will do so by providing what she has to offer in return, which is affection. The most faithful husband may turn to another woman if he is far from home and lonely, and if she is willing to accept him and the resources he has to offer her.

There were 66,000 babies fathered by allied soldiers in Germany after World War II. When under stress, humans quickly abandon the idea of monogamy.

2

The Monogamy Myth

Sometimes I wonder if men and women really suit each other. Perhaps they should live next door and just visit now and then.

KATHERINE HEPBURN

According to Edward O. Laumann, in *The Social Organization of Sexuality: Sexual Practices in the United States*, the average American man will have twelve sexual partners over the course of his lifetime, and the average American woman will have six partners. To some people, this may seem like promiscuous behavior. However, in primitive hunter-gatherer societies, men would have had sex at some time in their life with virtually every adult female in their community, and most women would have had sex with virtually every adult male. The modern American population studied by Laumann is certainly not monogamous, but "natural" human cultures make modern Americans seem prudish by comparison.

Monogamy is a good example of the conflict between human instincts and contemporary standards of behavior. Monogamy means having only one mate in a lifetime, the fairy-tale true love, the one and only soul mate. This is rare in the animal kingdom. There are a few monogamous species, notably snow geese, beavers, barn owls, prairie voles, and gray wolves. These creatures can choose a mate once in their adolescence, and can never do so again. They lack the ability to accept, or even consider an alternative mate. If a mate dies, the survivor never mates again. Humans are not like that.

I once had a patient, Mr. Johnston, who came to the ER for evaluation of chest pain. He was a rancher, and like many independent old men, he was not very adept at talking about his illness. He let his wife answer my questions. In the course of my interviewing her about his symptoms, she volunteered that he started having the chest pain when he discovered that she had been having an affair with one of the ranch hands. In the ER, we know very well that the sinking feeling a person gets in the middle of the chest during emotional trauma can be indistinguishable from the crushing pain of a heart attack. My cardiology instructor in medical school taught me that one of the causes of chest pain is a broken heart. Such was the case with Mr. Johnston. He was seventy-two years old, and his wife was seventy-one. Yet she had succumbed to a passionate extra-marital romance, and left him with a broken heart.

Human beings retain the capacity to fall in love and to succumb to lust throughout their lives, and long past their reproductive years. We humans monitor for alternative mates constantly, even when we are currently paired. We choose new mates easily, throughout life, at any age, even long past childbearing age. We typically go through multiple relationships in adolescence, before pairing for the purpose of child rearing. Once mated, we engage in countless fantasies involving people other than our mates. Some of these fantasies advance to extra-pair couplings, i.e., infidelity. A large proportion, perhaps a majority, of our long-term, child-rearing relationships end in dissolution. Most of us go on to choose new mates, and often remarry. True monogamy is rare among humans. We are not a monogamous species.

I have a colleague and friend named Josh who is a very masculine man, one of those men that just drip testosterone. He confided to me once that he did not understand some of his own behavior. He has a gorgeous wife who is great in bed and gives him all the sex that he wants, and yet he is always looking at other women and thinking about approaching them. Josh is under the impression that humans are monogamous, and that men look at other women only when their own wives fail to provide for their needs. In fact, humans constantly monitor for alternative mates regardless of their current status.

The Natural Forms of Human Families

The idea that one man and one woman can bond to form a lifelong partnership and "live happily ever after" is a fairly modern invention. The concept linking love and marriage originated in about the year 900 C.E., in the emerging culture of Christian Europe, when the first laws were passed restricting sex to marriage partners. Prior to that time, marriage was a business contract with political and economic obligations. It may have lasted a lifetime, but it had nothing to do with romance or emotional bonds. The purpose of marriage was to provide a legal basis for inheritance of property and power. Marriage also provided certain conjugal rights and obligations related to the production of legitimate heirs, but it was not exclusive. Romance, on the other hand, was extra-marital, between lovers and mistresses, or between adolescents, and was understood to be short-lived and ephemeral.

Under primitive conditions, humans naturally form three types of family models, and monogamy is not one of them. They are the polygyny model, the dioecious model, and the matrilineal model. All three are still present in various parts of the world, including most neighborhoods in Western societies, where they usually go unrecognized.

In the polygyny model, a man has multiple women as sexual partners. People often equate polygamy and harems, but harems are actually rare. They are restricted to a few ostentatiously wealthy and powerful men. Common polygamy consists of any man who is sexually active with two or more women at the same time, while those women are not sexually active with other men. The number of women he has is proportional to his wealth. These women serve him, and he provides for them. Polygamy is still officially sanctioned in about half the nations on Earth. It also persists unofficially in Western societies, where a wealthy man may have one or more mistresses in addition to his wife.

Carl is an executive in a high-paying position requiring frequent travel. He has an ex-wife to whom he pays alimony and child support for two children. He is currently married to his second wife, and has one child in that marriage. He also has several mistresses in different towns. I know one of the mistresses. She is married and has a child in that marriage. The uncertain paternity of the child has been the subject of community gossip. Carl represents the persistence of one of the primitive reproductive strategies. Here is a man who is sexually active with several women on an ongoing basis, a behavior made possible by his wealth and power. He is, for all practical purposes, polygynous.

In the dioecious model, which is Latin for "two houses," the men and women live in separate physical structures. Many indigenous peoples are dioecious. About half of the native cultures of North and South America lived in this manner prior to the arrival of Europeans. The women and young children live in one house, and the men live in another. When the male children become of age, they move to the men's house. Mating occurs between men and women sporadically or in brief relationships. The male parentage of the children is usually not known.

When I knew Deborah, she was twenty-two years old and a single mother, who had no contact with the father of her child. She shared a home with three other women, two of whom also had children. They all worked, and some were attending college. All the women were heterosexual and dated when they could. Mostly, they went to bars, although they occasionally met men through their work or school.

Deborah illustrates the persistence of the dioecious model for human reproductive behavior. The women and children live in one house. The men live somewhere else. The men and women meet each other out in the world sometimes and occasionally breed. Their relationships are sporadic and brief.

Dioecious families are seen all over the world today, wherever single women, some with their children, share a home, or several men share an apartment. Unwed humans generally prefer to share their homes with members of their own sex for a wide variety of reasons. It is unusual to find male and female co-habitants sharing sleeping quarters when they are not paired. Segregated college dormitories are officially sanctioned dioecious living arrangements. Even in the now popular coed dormitories, men and women share the same building, but not the same living quarters.

The matrilineal model is the most primitive and is still widely distributed. The female is bound to a home or a piece of land. She tends a garden and raises her children, who are the offspring of different men. Several men may occasionally visit her, bringing gifts in the form of meat or other resources to help her raise her children.

Each man will stay for a while, until he tires of the lifestyle or she tires of him and runs him off. But while they are together, they mate. He will not know which of her children are his, but while he is with her, he will assist in the support of all the children. Each of the men who spends time with the woman considers himself to be a father to all her children, and each of the children consider him to be one of their fathers. After he leaves one woman, he may go off to stay with another. And, soon, another man will appear to take his place.

Catherine is a patient of mine. I have, at various times, treated her, each of her four children, her mother, and her grandmother. She is thirty-two years old and has never been married. She and her children live with her mother and grandmother. The children have three different fathers. All three men are still present, off and on, and occasionally help with groceries and childrearing. She continues to be sexually active with all three men.

Catherine illustrates the persistence of the matrilineal model. These three men still provide resources to Catherine and help her raise the children, even though each of them does not know which, if any, of the children he has fathered. These men probably visit other women besides Catherine. From a reproductive point of view, they are now wasting their time and resources on Catherine, because she has had a tubal ligation and cannot produce any more children. Fortunately for her, their basic reproductive instincts are not affected by such technicalities. Human males will continue to provide resources to females who give sex, regardless of whether the females are fertile.

Catherine's family is matrilineal and matrilocal. That is, the children know who their female ancestors are, but not their male ancestors, and they live with their maternal relatives. They identify with their maternal family and have their mother's name. They can be certain of the identity of their mother and grandmother. The identity of their fathers is much less reliable, if it is known at all. Also, the home and children are in the possession of the females. The males are transients.

Monogamy may be the officially sanctioned family model for most of the world, but it does not occur naturally in humans. Modern humans try to maintain monogamous relationships, but they often fail. When this happens, it is insightful to observe the family models that develop spontaneously in the absence of the officially sanctioned model. When love fails, the most common family models people fall back on are dioecious, matrilineal, and polygynous.

Being Practical

Dr. Goldstein was having dinner with his wife in a posh restaurant when a stunning young blonde approached him, said, "Hi, Sammy." and kissed him, then walked away.

Mrs. Goldstein was shocked, and said, "Who was that?!"

The good doctor replied, "Oh that was my mistress."

"You have a mistress?! How long has this been going on?"

"Oh, about three years." he answered.

"Well! This is outrageous!" she said. "I want a divorce!"

"No you don't." he said. "Don't be silly. You've got it made. You don't have to work. Your kids are in private school. I buy you a new car every year."

At that moment, a gorgeous redhead walked up and said, "Hi, Sammy," kissed him, and walked away.

His wife said, "OK, and who was that?"

The good doctor responded, "Oh, that was Dr. Thompson's mistress."

Mrs. Goldstein replied, "Oh. I think ours is prettier." And returned to eating her meal.

3

The Purpose of Romantic Love

Where does the family start? It starts with a man falling in love with a girl.

Sir Winston Churchill

So, if we humans are not monogamous, then where does love come in to the picture? There are certainly times in our lives when we do have relationships that are strongly exclusive, if only for a short time. Humans form a special emotional bond called *love*. But *love* is a homonym. It is a nebulous term that refers to a wide range of thoughts and feelings. One can love a favorite dress, or a food, or a sport. One loves a spouse, or a pet. These are all different kinds of love, but they share a common theme, and it has something to do with the word *want*. People can love their work, their country, or their god, signifying devotion. People can make love, meaning they engage in sex. People can fall into a place or state called *love*.

Falling in love is something entirely different from *love*. It is not the act of loving, but rather the act of falling. When one falls in love, there is a sense of collapsing or descending into an emotional condition. There is a feeling of loss of control. This is why falling in love is sometimes compared to an illness. A person is referred to as "love-struck" or "lovesick."

In *The Road Less Traveled*, M. Scott Peck provides a very useful model of the emotional mechanics of falling in love. He describes it as an ego-boundary process. As a baby grows into a toddler and then into a child, she gradually learns that she is separate from the world and the people around her. She develops a sense of what is uniquely her self, her space, and her property. She learns that she has the ability to restrict the access of other persons to the things that are hers. She develops a sense of self.

As she grows older, through childhood into adolescence, she develops a sense of identity. She recognizes that she has a unique personality with her own ideas, desires, plans, wants, and needs. She forms an ego. She also learns her comfort level with other persons. She discovers, over time, how close she will let other people be to her, physically and emotionally. She learns how comfortable she is with sharing her space, her belongings, and her personal information. She develops ego boundaries.

But then, in early adulthood, something happens. This isolated person, wrapped in ego boundaries, meets someone whom she wants, and who wants her. As they approach each other, their ego boundaries rapidly collapse. As they grow closer, they begin to share their wants, desires, and plans. They share their space and their belongings. What is his is hers. What he wants, she wants. Whatever he wants to do, she wants to do, just to be with him. He will let her into his personal space and give her his belongings. She will let him into her personal space, let him get close to her, let him touch her body, even let him inside her body!

But how does this happen? What is going on in the body physiologically? A great deal of research is currently being done on the neurochemistry of romance. Two chemicals in the blood stream and the brain are at the forefront of this research. Oxytocin and dopamine are "feel-good" chemicals. They are associated with relaxation, joy, and contentment. Many other chemicals are involved, too. Falling in love is an ancient and complicated process. But the names of the chemicals are irrelevant. What is important is that there are measurable chemical changes that go on in the body when a person feels good.

When your lover smiles at you, or laughs at a joke, or compliments you, or touches your skin, it feels good because your body chemistry has been altered. When your lover kisses or caresses you, the levels of the feel-good chemicals in your blood stream and your brain rise. This is the reward you receive from a person who puts you at ease because you are attracted to him and because you sense that he is attracted to you. The more time you spend with this person, the more you feel at ease, and the more easily your body responds with outflows of the feel-good chemicals. When you are away from your lover, just thinking of that person causes the release of the chemicals.

In a very short time, this escalates into what could be best described as a catastrophic failure of your personal security system. Your ego boundaries completely collapse. You feel so good with your lover that you care about nothing else. You can think about nothing else. You are love struck and love sick.

Love is a grave mental disease.

PLATO

The two of you have fallen in love. You have merged your ego boundaries and think of yourselves as one entity. The two of you have become an "us," a "we." You want nothing except each other. You engage in magical thinking. As long as the two of you have each other, you want for nothing and you can overcome any hardship. You can climb mountains or swim seas to be together. Love will conquer all. You abandon your families, your homes, your plans, and your common sense in order to have each other. You cast aside all logic and all precaution. And, without logic or precaution, the two of you mate.

That is, of course, the whole point of it. Falling in love is the process that allows mating to take place. Without it, people would never get close enough to each other to mate. They are too protective of themselves. In the absence of love, people can experience occasional opportunistic sex, or violent rape, or other forms of loveless breeding, but they cannot create the sustained sexual activity of lovers that assures pregnancy or the sustained emotional bonds that nurture families. Both in conceiving and in raising young, those couples who fall in love have an advantage over those who do not.

He felt now that he was not simply close to her, but that he did not know where he ended and she began.

LEO TOLSTOY

4

The Down Side: Falling Out of Love

Sometimes you have to get to know someone really well to realize you're really strangers.

MARY TYLER MOORE

Biochemically, falling in love is no different for humans than it is for any other mammals. Hormones and chemicals in the brain and bloodstream cause us to relax so much that we allow our lovers to do things that we would never tolerate from anyone else. Consider the female cat, who, when in estrus, will let a male approach her, mount her, bite her on the head, and copulate with her. At any other time, she would not let him near her. Of course, the moment they complete the act, she turns and swats at him, indignant that he is in her personal space.

That is the problem with falling in love. It doesn't last. People inevitably fall out of love. Sometimes it takes years, and sometimes it takes a few hours, a truth reflected in the old song lyric, "What are you going to do in the morning, when that cowboy don't get up and go home?"

At the beginning, falling in love is easy and effortless. It is, after all, falling. But eventually it starts to require some work. When two people have fallen in love, each tries to be what he thinks the other wants, but no one can keep that up for very long. As the novelty of the situation wears off, the level of feel-good chemicals starts to fall. Eventually, the ego boundaries start to come back up, and the two persons start to separate. Each starts to protect his own space. Their individual wants and desires re-emerge. She wants to watch TV, but he wants to have sex. He wants to see an action flick, and she wants to watch a chick flick. She wants to redecorate, and he wants to spend the money on a hunting trip. They have become individuals again. The courtship has ended. The honeymoon is over.

New lovers are dominated by positive emotional experiences. Their physical bodies are awash in the feel-good chemicals that fuel their desire for each other. But as they spend time together, they have negative experiences, too. When enough of these accumulate, the actions that once triggered release of oxytonin, instead cause release of adrenaline, the famed hormone of the "fight or flight response." The lover's touch or the request for a gift is no longer pleasurable, but becomes an annoyance.

"I love being married. It's so great to find that one special person you want to annoy for the rest of your life."

Rita Rudner

Jokes like these thrive in the popular culture because we can identify with them. We are sympathetic to the characters. We have a certain familiarity with their situations. We all know that in extended pairs, the bliss of love fades away, and the relationship between the ex-lovers eventually becomes adversarial.

"Love is temporary insanity, curable by marriage"

Ambrose Bierce

There is a universally recognized undercurrent of cynicism that relates to long-term human relationships. We all know that the bliss of romance fades and people get tired of each other. Lovers eventually go back to being people with their own separate agendas. Countless song lyrics lament the transience of romance. Think of "April, Come She Will" by Simon and Garfunkel, or "You Don't Bring Me Flowers Anymore" and "Solitary Man" by Neil Diamond. Poetry and lyrics that expound upon the failure of romantic love are popular because they speak to the experiences of almost everyone.

No wonder young people are confused about love. Half of our love songs praise the resilience and permanence of love, while the other half lament love's ephemeral nature and fragility. Our romantic narratives talk of the bliss of never-ending love, while our humor exploits the implausibility of permanent devotion. It is all very confusing.

What Was the Question?

A human physiology lecturer notices that he is losing the attention of his class, so, to try to wake them up, he singles out a woman in the front row, and asks, "Do you know what your asshole is doing when you're having an orgasm?"

She responds, "He's usually out playing golf with his buddies."

Anon.

False Expectations

> "Marriage is like putting your hand into a bag of snakes in the hope of pulling out an eel."
>
> LEONARDO DA VINCI

Young people go into their relationships thinking they will live happily-ever-after with their one true love. Then, as love wanes, their feelings get hurt. It is just the ego boundaries coming back up, but that is not how it looks to the two lovers. Each of them has made promises to the other that they cannot keep. Each feels betrayed by the other. Each feels that the other either lied about their feelings in the first place or has changed the way they feel. Of course, they have changed, and they did lie. It is not called lying, but it certainly is misinformation. Women don't lie to their lovers. They just "make sacrifices for the sake of the relationship." Men don't lie either. They call it "courting." But the truth is that she doesn't like to have sex during primetime TV. And the truth is, he doesn't like chick flicks. And the fact is, each of them did deceive the other.

In Agreement

After a quarrel, a husband said to his wife, "You know, I was a fool when I married you."

She replied, "Yes, dear, but I was in love, and I didn't notice."

Anon.

So now they find themselves in a relationship that is not following the script they studied. They have read the fairy tales, watched the romantic films, and studied the dogma of their religion. They have each learned their parts and played them correctly, but they are not living happily-ever-after. They find themselves fighting an uphill battle against reality, armed only with their unrealistic expectations. And yet, there is nothing wrong with their relationship. It is just following its natural course. The problem is not their relationship, but their expectations.

As they gradually become more disillusioned with the relationship, they go through a well-defined progression of stages. At first, the lovers are contented. But as the disappointment accumulates, they begin to complain. When that fails to correct the situation, they advance to criticism. And, when things have gone far enough, they turn to contempt.

Contentment:	"We're so in love, we don't need to go out anywhere."
Complaining:	"I wish we could go out to the movies sometime."
Criticizing:	"You never take me to a movie anymore."
Contempt:	"You never take me out anymore, you cheap bastard."

From Gottman, J. (1995)

At the same time, both go through the standard grieving process originally described by Elizabeth Kubler-Ross. They have each lost something important. They have lost that feeling of being in love, that sensation of bliss, that special relationship. And they grieve. They go through the standard progression of denial, anger, bargaining, depression, and acceptance. Acceptance is the ultimate goal because, once that stage is reached, they can get on with their real purpose of raising a family. However, there are dangers along the way, and many grieving lovers never reach the stage of acceptance.

The Stages of Grief for Relationships

Denial

"This is just a phase we're going through."
"He's just stressed out about his work (school, parents, health)."
"She's just not feeling well lately." "We're just taking a time out."

Anger:

"I really hate it when he does this."
"She's cut me off just to piss me off."
"I'll be damned if he's getting into my pants anymore."
(Of course, this is where the lawyers make their money. If they get their claws into a couple at this stage, they will fan the flames of condescension until this natural anger becomes demonic hatred.)

Bargaining:

He agrees not to ask for sex until her TV programs are over. She concedes that he can go hunting. (This is a genuine attempt by one or both parties to negotiate, offering concessions and voicing their needs. Marriage counselors make their money by facilitating this process.)

Depression:

The bargaining makes peace, but it does not bring back the lost feelings. Apathy sets in. He drinks too much. She stays in bed all day. They turn to others for sympathy and understanding.

Acceptance:

Both parties settle in to the realization that the original romance is gone forever. They set aside their feelings and disappointments, accept their situation, and get back to the tasks of raising the kids and paying the bills.

Sadly, the lovers both feel that they have failed. Their love has not lived up to their expectations. They have "settled" into a life-long obligation with someone whom they now believe is not their one true love. They do not understand how it happened, and each harbors the grudge that this is the other's fault. Each feels shame for what he perceives as his own bad choices, guilt for the way he has acted toward his partner, and resentment for the way he has been treated. Of course, the fault lies not in the lovers' actions, but in their original expectations. They thought they would remain deeply in love, living happily-ever-after. But that is not what humans do.

Wounded by the perceived failure of their relationship, and isolated from each other by their hurt feelings, the two lovers are not able to see that they have actually succeeded by reaching this point. Their ego boundaries have reformed, and they are now two separate individuals again. It is time for them to move on to the next level.

The Next Level

Only after two people fall out of love can they start to build a viable long-term relationship. That may seem like an odd thing to say, but consider this: a mature stable relationship must accommodate the needs of the individuals involved, but before two people fall out of love, they are not acting as separate individuals. Until their ego boundaries reform, they are not able to think of themselves as independent persons. They cannot express their individual needs. They will make concessions that they will regret later. They will make promises that they cannot keep. An old adage says, "Never believe anything your lover tells you in bed." Until they fall out of love, it is just the hormones talking.

A sustainable long-term relationship must be a co-nurturing process in which the two lovers help each other to grow as individuals while they work together toward common goals. That cannot happen until they have gone through the ecstasy of ego merging and the agony of ego separation. Too often, lovers reach this point and are swamped with disillusionment. They feel betrayed by their partners and entrapped by their own promises.

Enlightened lovers focus on helping each other through this process, instead of blaming each other for it. They recognize that relationships change over time and evolve from hormonal to intellectual. They work together to build a partnership that can survive the challenges that time will bring.

My parents were married for sixty years. My maternal grandparents were married for seventy years, and my paternal grandparents for about that same number. I have countless friends who adore their spouses long after their original pair bonds expired. I have also known countless people who ended up adoring their ex-spouses.

My colleague, John, was a busy physician with a wife and two children. He and his wife had known each other since high school and had married young. His marriage was chronically in turmoil, to the extent that it often interfered with his work. His wife would come to the office, and they would have loud quarrels. He ultimately divorced her, but stayed around to help raise the children. Within a year, he was living with her again. They co-habitated for years, but never re-married. If they had any further conflict, it was never evident. During this time, they both dated other people. They stayed together for another decade, and finally separated again after the children were old enough to move out. John died after a long illness. His ex-wife cared for him during the illness and was at his bedside when he died.

John and his wife got along well after they divorced. Once they had been relieved of the pressure to act as if they were still in love, and they accepted that their passion was gone, they were able to get on with their lives. They renewed the friendship they had known since their teenage years and attended to the tasks of raising their children and taking care of each other.

The Post-Romantic Relationship

John and his ex-wife are a good example of an effective post-romantic relationship. Sustained long-term relationships are necessary today, simply because the structure of human society is so different now. Primitive family structures were adequate for humans when life was primitive. Population density was lower. People did not move frequently. They lived out their lives in villages surrounded by extended family. Their children were raised by the village around them. Most of a child's education came from other members of the village. The body of human knowledge was small and could be learned by casual association.

Today's children are not immersed in a village of intimate friends and relatives. In all but the most rural places on Earth, children today are surrounded by strangers. Their rearing depends upon a strong nuclear-family unit. On the other hand, human culture has advanced to the point that each person owns only a tiny fraction of the body of human knowledge, and everyone needs formal education to understand the basic rules of society. An informal education cannot provide for the needs of modern children or modern cultures. It now takes eighteen years or more to teach children everything they need to know.

A complex, costly behavior pattern such as monogamy cannot persist in a population unless it offers some survival advantage. Monogamy persists in human societies because it provides the benefit of extended nurturing by two parents. People try to be monogamous because it is the best way to raise healthy, well-educated children in a modern technological culture. Likewise, societies and cultures try to convince people to be monogamous because that is what is best for those societies and cultures.

We have now come back around to the question that I asked my junior colleague Caroline. Why would she allow men to overrule the instructions given to her by God through her genetic code? It is because she lives in a modern world. She does not live in a primitive society. She believes that her son will thrive better in a two-parent patriarchal household.

She has this belief because it has been taught to her by her parents, society, and culture. She has also been taught by her religion that it is the natural role of a woman to be subservient to one man throughout her lifetime. And so she does not understand why it does not feel right for her.

It is vitally important that people recognize that it is not natural for humans to form lifelong, monogamous relationships any more than it is natural for humans to take medicines, or to sit long hours in classrooms. Lovers should understand in advance that monogamy is an artificial behavior that has a purpose, but is difficult and uncomfortable for humans. Only then can they avoid the feelings of guilt, shame, and resentment that destroy an intimate relationship. When falling out of love results in hurt feelings, it takes all the joy out of the relationship. But if lovers understand that falling out of love is part of the natural progression in a relationship, they have a much better chance of retaining their original intimacy as they graduate into a mature, nurturing partnership.

Making that transition is tough. A mature partnership is a completely different emotional arrangement from the bond shared by a couple who have only recently fallen in love. It is held together by an entirely different set of instinctive behaviors that have little to do with romance. When applied to post-romantic relationships, the word *love*, has little to do with passion. The expression "I love you," ceases to mean, "I have the hots for you," and starts to mean, "I still plan to be your social partner for the long-term." There may be a place for passion and intimacy, but the couples that succeed in constructing durable long-term relationships will be those who recognize the value of good friendship and the golden rule.

Romantic love is transient. It does not last long enough to raise children to adulthood. The rearing of children in a modern society requires a partnership and friendship that extends far beyond the natural duration of the romantic bonds that humans form.

"I don't think I'll get married again. I'll just find a woman I don't like, and buy her a house."

Louis Grizzard

5

Pair Bonds

Love is only a dirty trick played on us to achieve continuation of the species.

W. Somerset Maugham

If humans are not naturally monogamous, then why do they fall in love? Falling in love is not without costs. It is emotionally, socially, and economically expensive. Both members of a pair put their resources and their reputations at risk. Helen Fisher, PhD, an anthropologist at Rutgers University, writes in *Anatomy of Love* that falling in love is similar to the seasonal pair-bonding that occurs in birds and other animals. It lasts only for a set period, related to the time required for raising a brood. Humans can reproduce without pair bonds, but the pair bond performs several important functions in human reproduction.

Pair bonding is the dominant strategy programmed into human genes, but in the modern world, it is not the best way to raise children. The duration of the pair bond is too short. The most effective parenting relationship is an extended pairing, called marriage, which lasts long enough to raise children to adulthood. However, this requires couples to remain together long past the end of their natural pair bond.

The term *serial monogamy* is a poor substitute for *pair bonding*. First, it is an oxymoron. Monogamy means one mate for life, and serial monogamy violates that definition. Second, serial monogamy implies that human relationships are exclusive, which they are not. The situation is much more complex than that. Virtually all modern societies have rules that encourage people to enter into lifelong marital arrangements that include an obligation to fidelity, and there are good reasons for doing so. But, a large proportion of people fail to follow those rules, by chance or by choice. This is because humans are simply not by nature monogamous. They are naturally inclined to have both romantic and sexual interactions with people other than their mates.

Pair-bonding is a more accurate descriptive term for the natural form of human reproductive relationships. This means that two individuals join together for the purpose of cooperatively raising a brood of offspring. The pair bond lasts for the length of one breeding cycle. Most birds do this. So do a few mammals, and even a few fish, but birds are the best example. The male and female join for a single season to mate, build a nest, hatch the eggs, and nurture the young.

For centuries, nesting birds have been admired as models of monogamy. Under the scrutiny of modern science, though, they have fallen from grace. Virtually every one of the passerine (perching) birds studied thus far, and these comprise more than half of all bird species, turn out to be unfaithful to their mates to some degree. Careful DNA analysis of the droppings from under nests show that up to forty percent of chicks are not the offspring of the male that helped raise them. Furthermore, with rare exception, pairs of birds separate after the brood is raised, and never see each other again. Even among the most faithful species, such as mourning doves, a pair will abandon each other and the nest they have built if they do not produce an egg in a timely fashion.

The work done by Helen Fisher and reported in her book, *Anatomy of Love*, provides a compelling argument that Homo sapiens is a pair-bonding species. Her transcultural studies of divorce rates demonstrate a peak after four to seven years of marriage. Humans are naturally inclined to change mates after that much time together. Under natural conditions, the human male and female form a union that typically lasts four to seven years and allows the rearing of one or two children through weaning. The couple then separates, and both parties go on to find other mates and raise additional families.

Under natural conditions, each adult typically forms four or five such unions over the course of a lifetime, and has one or two children per bond. In most primitive cultures, both the male and the female are free to engage in extra-pair couplings while pair-bonded. In fact, many primitive cultures encourage both parties to have multiple partners.

The same pattern still persists in modern societies around the world. More than half of marriages end in divorce, usually after four to seven years, and most divorced people remarry. Despite admonitions against extra-marital sex and despite the social pressure to remain monogamous, modern American females have an average of six sexual partners during their lifetimes, while males have about twice this number.

Furthermore, despite sanctions against, and sometimes strict penalties for, extramarital sex, fifty percent of women and seventy percent of men engage in extra-pair couplings at some point in their lives. Clearly, modern humans are no more inclined than their primitive ancestors to have exclusive sexual relationships. From the dawn of history, they have habitually sought sexual partners outside their primary unions. It is basic human nature.

One would expect human beings to become better at a task with practice. If they are monogamous by nature, and are trying to be monogamous in their relationships, then divorce rates should fall in subsequent marriages. This is not the case. First marriages have a fifty-percent divorce rate. Most of these divorcees will remarry, and the divorce rate for the second marriages will be seventy percent. The divorce rates for third marriages will be eighty percent. What is going on here? Practice clearly does not make people better at being married. Rather, it seems to make them better at divorcing. Perhaps they simply become more adept at recognizing when to quit a relationship that has exhausted the pair bond. The result, though, is that no matter how hard they try to be monogamous, most humans end up with a life history of a series of pair bonds.

Human beings are pair-bonders. They fall in love, stay in love long enough to raise one or two children past weaning, and then fall out of love. Their pair bond lasts for the time that their ego-boundaries are down. When a couple falls out of love, when their ego-boundaries come back up and their pair bond ends, they are genetically programmed to abandon their relationship and find new partners.

Why do fools fall in love? Why do they fall in love?

Frankie Lymon

What, then, is the point of the pair bond? Humans have evolved, or have been designed, to fall in love. They go to all the trouble of forming a special relationship with one individual of the opposite sex, only to cheat on that person, and eventually to separate. If the pair bond is transient and non-exclusive, then what adaptive purpose does it serve? Why don't people just choose mates on an intellectual, political, economic, or random basis? Well, in fact, many cultures do just that. They arrange marriages without any input from the two parties who are bound by the arrangement. And, intriguingly, their divorce rates are much lower than those in Western cultures. So, why do people fall in love?

Perhaps falling in love is a reliable way to choose the best mate for lifelong love, support, and the rearing of children. But this is doubtful. People fall in love with the most inappropriate persons. They fall in love with people who are already pair-bonded, or who are incapable of bonding. They fall in love with persons who could never possibly raise or support a family, people who are grossly irresponsible, chronically destitute, or in prison. Women fall in love with men who killed their previous wives, and men fall in love with women who demonize their three previous husbands. Men fall in love with men, and women fall in love with women. We will investigate the role of homosexuality in childrearing in great detail later, but for now, I am just making the point that falling in love is far from infallible as a method for choosing the perfect mate for propagating the species.

Perhaps falling in love is a means to identify a mate who is appropriate for a person's social network, but evidence is to the contrary. In fact, it may do just the opposite. People fall in love with others who are totally at odds with their social network. They often search outside their local social circle for mates. They find themselves in love with persons not of their races, outside their religions, vastly above or below their social stations, totally outside their age ranges, and completely unacceptable to their parents and families. The classic love stories share a common theme of impossible loves between members of different social classes, as in *Cinderella*, or warring factions, as in *Romeo and Juliet*.

Perhaps falling in love guarantees that one will live "happily-ever-after." Again, the evidence argues against it. The pair bond is clearly a short-lived phenomenon. People fall out of love. The honeymoon ends. Fairy tales are filled with couples who live out their lives together in bliss from their first kiss in adolescence, but in real life the bookstore shelves are filled with volumes advising people on how to struggle through marriage after the honeymoon ends.

So, the title question remains unanswered: Why do humans fall in love and form pair bonds as their preferred mating strategy? This must somehow be adaptive. It must provide some advantage to the lovers and their progeny or the behavior would not persist in the population. People would not be made this way unless it served some purpose.

Humans can reproduce without falling in love, but falling in love expedites and fine-tunes mating in several important ways that aid in human survival. First, it allows two persons to be lovers, and to create offspring. That is, it allows their ego boundaries to collapse so that the two separate individuals, each with their own personal space, can trust each other enough and get close enough to become lovers. It expedites mating and the mixing of gametes, the joining of sperm and ovum.

Of course, women can get pregnant without falling in love. There are hundreds of other reasons for having sex besides being in love, and all of them can result in pregnancy. Women can submit to loveless sex in an arranged marriage. They can trade sex for resources or opportunities. They can be artificially inseminated, or engage in hedonistic orgies. But the great majority of pregnancies are the result of two persons knowing and trusting each other well enough to merge their personal spaces, remove their clothing, make bodily contact, and lose themselves in the passion of loving until their gametes mix. That requires the level of trust that comes with pair-bonding.

Secondly, the pair bond is advantageous for humans, just as it is for many other animals that have extremely infantile, dependent offspring. Pregnancy and nursing are a burden to the human female, limiting her ability to provide for herself and her children. She is dependent on a mate to help her until her children can walk and can feed themselves. Those female human ancestors who could attract and hold the devotion of a partner had more resources to care for their babies. They had more food, shelter, and protection than a single mother, and more of their offspring survived. The same is true of the males who stayed with their mates and helped in the raising of their young. Their children had a higher survival rate than the offspring of non-pair-bonding males.

Finally, pair bonding paradoxically restricts humans to relatively unfamiliar persons in their choices for mates. Humans cannot fall into romantic love with people they already know well. This is called the Westermark effect, after the man who first noted that people who are raised as children in the same household never fall in love as adults, even if they are unrelated. This has been confirmed repeatedly, especially in the setting of communes in the second half of the 1900s, where children raised communally rarely chose marriage partners from their own communes.

Humans are not able to drop their ego boundaries and merge with other individuals whom they know too well. There has to be some mystery about a person in order for love interest to occur. Perhaps people who know each other well cannot deceive themselves into overlooking each other's faults, and cannot deceive each other regarding their intentions and desires. Love is blind, and apparently blindness is a prerequisite for love. It is physically possible for a brother and sister to engage in sex, but they are not inclined to do so. Their ego boundaries prevent it. They cannot get that close without being offended by each other's presence in their personal space. The pair-bonding process inhibits incestuous romance.

For the same reason, pair-bonding reduces population inbreeding and promotes genetic mixing. In primitive tribal societies, pair-bonding causes adolescents to move from one clan to another. They are more inclined to choose a mate from outside their circle of family and close friends than from within. Girls are more interested in boys from the next village, rather than the boys they grew up with.

Of course, the corollary to this is that familiarity breeds contempt, and after people get to know each other too well, they fall out of love. The period of blissful ignorance expires. The pair bond starts to dissolve. Unlike birds, though, human children do not abruptly leave the nest at the end of the pair bond. The end point of the relationship in humans is not clear-cut. Instead, the couples drift apart. They lose interest in each other, get annoyed with each other, and start looking at alternatives. That is, they begin to stray.

Reproductive Strategies

David Buss and David Schmitt, from the Department of Psychology, University of Michigan, have described human mating strategies in a way that explains the human inclination to cheat. Their model separates human mating behavior into four separate strategies, two for the males and two for the females. Each of these strategies has certain problems to be solved, rules to be followed, rewards to be gained, and risks to be incurred.

Pair-bonding is the core of the long-term strategy for both the male and the female, but the sexes are genetically programmed to have different concerns when choosing a long-term partner. Males and females judge potential mates according to different criteria, reflecting their opposing needs. Recall that the female has a relatively small number of opportunities for reproduction in her lifetime, compared to the male, and each of her offspring will require a large investment on her part. She will have greater reproductive success in the long run if she is very selective. She strives for the greatest amount of commitment and support, as well as the highest quality genetic material. Note that the support and the genetic material do not have to come from the same male. In contrast, the male has an endless supply of gametes to put wherever he has the opportunity, with potentially no further investment on his part. He enhances his reproductive success by forming a pair bond supporting the mother of his children, but he has other options that are not available to females.

When searching for a long-term mate, a male must locate and woo an available female. He must overcome the competition from other males for her attention. The female he chooses must be fertile, but not already pregnant. She must be in good health, young enough to raise a family, and not overly burdened with children from previous mating. She must have good parenting skills. She must possess good genetic material, which he will judge by her attractiveness.

She should be difficult to coax into bed, which indicates that she will resist short-term mating liaisons with other males. Chastity is desirable in a long-term partner, because it decreases the likelihood of infidelity. But she must be attainable. She must be willing to pair bond with him in return for the resources and commitment he can offer, so that he is not wasting his time. That is to say, she has to want him, too. He is not likely to pursue a woman with higher social station or earning power.

A woman searching for a long-term mate must locate and attract a man who has resources that will persist over a period of time long enough for her to raise a child. He must be willing to pair bond with her and to commit those resources to her and her offspring. He should be physically able to protect her and her children, but must not be a threat to them. He must also be tolerant of any children she may have from previous mating. And he must have good-quality genes, which she will judge by his attractiveness.

The attractiveness of the long-term mate is of less importance to a woman than to a man. This is because a woman has the option of obtaining the genetic material for her offspring from a man who is not her partner. She can pair bond with a good provider and then utilize extra-pair couplings to obtain genetic material for her offspring. That is, she can cheat on her partner by having a more attractive lover on the side. In fact, that is the core of the short-term mating strategy for females. Alternatively, she can choose a long-term partner for her protection and support after she is already pregnant. This is not saying that women are all inclined to cheat on their husbands, but rather that women are hardwired to put more emphasis on earning power than on attractiveness when looking for a long-term mate.

A woman desires earning power in a long-term mate, but she can obtain insemination from a higher-quality (better-looking) male if she does not restrict her choices to men who are willing to support her. Good-looking men are a dime a dozen if the only commitment required from the man is the price of dinner and a bottle of wine. If she is willing to take the risks, a woman can have the best of both worlds. She can pair bond with a male who has resources to commit to her offspring, and still combine her genes with those of a more attractive male who is not willing to support her. If she succeeds, her spouse is none the wiser and expends his resources on another man's offspring. Remember, genes are selfish.

When one man impregnates another man's wife, the traditional name for this is "cuckolding," after a family of birds, the cuckoos, who lay their eggs in the nests of other birds. The cuckoo egg hatches earlier than the host's eggs, and the cuckoo chick pushes the rightful eggs out of the nest. The owners of the nest do not recognize that the sole remaining chick in the nest is not their own species, and they feed it until it grows to maturity and flies away to parasitize some other hapless couple.

Cuckolding happens commonly in humans. With modern blood typing, tissue typing, and DNA sequencing techniques, paternity is no longer a mystery. It has become a simple matter to determine whether the father of a woman's child is, in fact, her husband. Depending on the study one reads, three to eleven percent of children born to married women are the product of extra-pair couplings. That is, the genetic father is not the woman's husband. Most people are not surprised by those statistics, because they know that both men and women are genetically programmed to seek out opportunistic extra-pair couplings for the enhancement of their reproductive success.

The short-term mating strategy for men is completely different from women. Human males are genetically programmed to spread their seed around wherever they can. When men go searching for opportunistic mating partners, the main emphasis is on availability, while attractiveness is much less important. The pair-bonded male who seeks additional females does so with no intention of making any investment in the offspring beyond the initial bottle of wine, or a fresh-caught fish, or some honeycomb, or even a one-hundred-dollar bill. He trades resources for an opportunistic coupling, and then he is gone. He has lots of gametes to spare and very low biological risk.

A Late-Night Surprise

Bubba was walking home from the bar late one night and saw the outline of a woman in the shadows. "Twenty dollars" she whispers.

Bubba had never been with a hooker before, but decides what the hell, it's only twenty bucks. So he goes into the bushes and meets her. They're 'engaged' for a few minutes when all of a sudden a light flashes on them. It is a police officer. "What's going on here, people?" asks the officer.

"I'm making love to my wife!" Bubba answers, sounding annoyed.

"Oh, I'm sorry," says the cop, "I didn't know."

"Well, neither did I, 'til ya shined that light in her face."

****

Sometimes it seems that the more offensive a joke is, the more it reveals about human nature.

Here are a husband and wife whose pair bond is near or past its end. He has left her unattended while he goes out to a bar for the evening, searching for entertainment and short-term mating opportunities with other women.

He succeeds in finding what he believes to be an opportunity for an extra-pair coupling. Only after the police officer shines a light on her face, does he realize that the woman he has paid for sex is actually his wife.

The reader is left to assume that the wife was equally surprised. She was left unattended by her husband, and took advantage of his absence to seek out her own short-term mating opportunities. Her purpose was entirely different from his. She simply wanted to obtain resources in exchange for sex, presumably planning to keep her earnings secret from her husband.

They both thought that they had succeeded, only to find that fate had crossed their paths, causing them to collide. In one fell swoop, their efforts were foiled, their misbehaviors were exposed to each other, and they were both busted.

A gallivanting male would prefer short-term mating with a highly attractive female if one is available, but such a woman is likely to require more resources from him, and more of his time, before she submits to copulation. This not only costs him resources, but he also incurs the risk of being cuckolded himself. The more time he is away from his mate, the more opportunity she has to stray or to entertain another male.

The offspring of a gallivanting male would benefit most if he impregnates a female who is pair-bonded to a man with resources. They would be raised well and would fare better than if the female was unsupported. Cuckoldry is a viable reproductive strategy. In fact, it is the entire strategy for a whole genus of birds, the Cuckoos. But cuckoldry is not without risks. The gallivanting male may be discovered, if the mate of his chosen amour is practicing competent mate-guarding. Jealousy over mates has always been and still is one of the most

Weee bit

An extraordinarily handsome man decided he had a responsibility to marry the perfect woman, so they could produce beautiful children beyond comparison. With that as his mission, he began searching for the perfect wife. Shortly thereafter, he met a farmer who had three stunning daughters who positively took his breath away.

He explained his mission to the farmer, asking for permission to marry one of them. The farmer simply replied, "They're lookin' to get married, so you came to the right place. Look 'em over and pick the one you want." The man had a date with the first daughter. The next day the farmer asked for his opinion.

"Well," said the man, "she's just a weeeeee bit ... not that you can hardly notice ... pigeon-toed." The farmer nodded and suggested the man date one of the other girls, so the man went out with the second daughter. The next day, the farmer again asked how things went.

"Well," the man replied, "she's just a weeeee bit ... not that you can hardly tell ... cross-eyed." The farmer nodded and suggested he date the third girl to see if things might be better. So he did.

The next morning, the man rushed in exclaiming, "She's perfect, just perfect. She's the one I want to marry." So they were wed right away, and in no time at all they were expecting a child. Months later, the baby was born. When the man visited the nursery, he was horrified: the baby was the ugliest, most pathetic human you can imagine. He rushed to his father-in-law, asking how such a thing could happen considering the beauty of the parents.

"Well," explained the farmer, "when you met her, she was just a weeeee bit ... not that you could hardly tell ... pregnant."

The obvious truth in this joke is that the man who marries a woman and supports her need not be the same as the man who impregnates her.

What makes this joke so funny, though, in my opinion, is the sudden reversal of fortunes of this arrogant young man at the hands of his father-in-law, his wife, and her two sisters. He judged these three young women based only on their physical beauty, remaining completely oblivious to matters of much greater importance. His superficial assessment skills made it easy for his future in-laws to manipulate him into marrying the girl who was already pregnant. Now he has been cuckolded.

common causes of homicide among human males. Even today, some states in the U.S. still allow a "crime of passion" defense. That is, the courts will excuse a man for killing another man he finds with his wife. In primitive societies such as the Kalihari Bushmen of southern Africa, the incidence of homicide among the males is thirty percent. That is to say, three out of ten adult males die from homicide. The most common cause of conflict resulting in homicide is jealousy. Mating can be a dangerous game.

A few years ago, a local attorney, fifty-four years old, married, and the father of three adult children, came to me with facial injuries and a broken nose after being assaulted by the husband of his mistress. She was forty, and a mother of two grown children, but looked much younger and was very pretty. She was a paralegal, working for the attorney, and they had been having an affair that was widely discussed by the gossips in the legal community. Her husband worked out of town on alternate weeks, which gave her ample time to play. Eventually, the husband discovered the affair and went to the attorney's office where the two of them had a verbal confrontation that escalated into a fistfight. The attorney clearly lost the fight. Even today among civilized, well-educated people, jealousy over females is a common cause of violence among men. Every human male has the instinct to kill a rival male over the issue of access to a female. In less civilized times and places, this confrontation might well have ended in murder.

The risk-benefit ratio for infidelity is completely different for males and females, and dictates different behaviors for optimal survival. The female stands to benefit from higher quality genetic material to mix with her own when conceiving her offspring. She also stands to gain resources or favors from an additional male. However, she risks offending her current pair-bonded mate and losing her source of support if he questions her devotion or the paternity of her offspring. She will be inclined to engage in extra-pair couplings only with males she finds more attractive or more resourceful than her mate, and she will do so selectively and discreetly.

The human female has little to gain biologically from a large number of sexual partners. She does not get additional offspring or any increase in the propagation of her genes. She is limited to one pregnancy about every two years or so, no matter how much she has sex. She benefits from the support of a devoted mate who will assist her during pregnancy and lactation and she uses affection to hold that mate. However she may still benefit from extra-pair couplings. She may gain pleasure, resources, food, social status, or opportunities. But unlike the male, she realizes no advantage from extra-pair couplings that have no strings attached. Like Bubba's wife, the pair-bonded female engages in infidelity for the extra resources and support she receives. She is genetically programmed to accept lovers who either show some commitment to her, or are more attractive than her long-term mate. That is to say that, unlike the male, she will not give it away. She will be much more selective than a male.

In contrast, the male has the potential to benefit from every extra-pair coupling. Every tryst may result in an additional offspring, and an additional copy of the male's genes in the gene pool, requiring no further investment on his part. Males are so inclined not because they foresee the value of additional offspring, but rather because males with this characteristic have historically had more offspring. So most men are now hardwired to couple with any female, regardless of her attractiveness, as long as she is available. Men may prefer chastity in long-term mates, but they want a short-term mate to be easy. The cheaper, the better. The only risks they incur are the loss of the resources they expend, and any personal dangers they incur. They will be discreet only when it is required to protect their own safety. In fact, if a man is highly attractive, he may benefit from advertising his availability. Pair-bonded females with unattractive mates will seek him out. Professional sports figures are notorious for the use of this strategy in attracting females.

Summary

People fall in love as a means of forming pair bonds with breeding partners who come from outside the circle of their own families. Both males and females are genetically programmed to form pair bonds as their long-term mating strategy. The term of the bond is generally four to seven years. A male looks to form a pair bond with a female who is healthy, attractive, and able to raise children. A female looks for a male who is healthy, attractive, and able to protect and provide for her and her children. Both males and females are also genetically programmed to seek short-term mating opportunities outside of their pair bond. Males are programmed to take advantage of any opportunity to copulate with any available female. Females are programmed to discretely and selectively have sex with males who offer resources or opportunities in return for sex, or who are more attractive than the male who is their current mate. That is the core of human reproductive strategies. Everything else is just variations on that theme.

Historical note

The current master of human cuckoldry is a physician named Cecil Jacobson, who ran a fertility clinic in the suburbs of Washington, D.C. in the 1970s. His practice consisted primarily of artificially inseminating women who were married to infertile men. The services he provided were not covered by medical insurance, and his clients were all wealthy enough to pay out of pocket. Dr. Jacobson told his clients that he used semen from a local sperm bank. However, the enterprising doctor reduced his overhead costs by using his own semen. By the time one of the couples noticed that their child resembled the doctor, he had successfully treated the infertility of seventy-five women. Dr. Jacobson committed an astounding array of ethical and legal offenses. Nonetheless, he enjoys tremendous reproductive success. He has fathered seventy-five offspring, all of whom will be raised by affluent pair-bonded couples.

6

What Is Attractive

Mr. Winwood Reade, however, who has had ample opportunities for observation, not only with the negroes of the West Coast of Africa, but with those of the interior who have never associated with Europeans, is convinced that their ideas of beauty are ON THE WHOLE the same as ours.

CHARLES DARWIN, *THE DESCENT OF MAN*

What do people look for in a mate? To both sexes, *attractive* means physical beauty, symmetry of facial features, good posture, clear skin, absence of physical deformity, and other evidence of good general health. It also includes the absence of foul odors and foul dispositions. A nice smile, a pleasant voice, and cheerful mood are important to both men and women. No one likes someone who is blatantly offensive in his or her appearance, odor, or personality. Beyond that, both males and females are hard-wired to like certain things in a mate.

What do Men Want?

A human male is genetically programmed to prefer certain physical characteristics in a female. Breasts are necessary for nursing offspring, and are physical evidence of the female's ability to care for infants. Likewise, wide hips are evidence of the female's ability to deliver babies and survive childbirth. Smooth body contours are evidence of her state of nutrition. Healthy women have a layer of fat under their skin that represents a storehouse of food, which they will mobilize to produce milk for their offspring.

The human male also desires a female with a narrow waist. This may seem paradoxical because it limits a man's choices to women with relatively low body fat. But this is not so much a matter of what he wants in a woman, as what he does not want. The narrow waist excludes most women who are already pregnant. A reproductively successful male does not expend his time, resources, and gametes on a female who is already pregnant by someone else. This is not for any cognitive reason. Basic instincts do not rely on intellect. It is simply because men who exercised such discretion propagated more of their genes than men who did not, and after millennia, most men now have that disposition. Men favor women with a waist:hip ratio of 7:10, whether they are in the African bush, the southern tip of South America, the Asian Steppes, the Australian Outback, or New York City. On all continents, and in all cultures and races, men prefer women with an hourglass figure.

Men also instinctively seek women who are young. When a man impregnates a woman, he procures her services for the rest of her life in caring for his child and propagating his genes. The younger a female is, the more years she has available to dedicate to his progeny. A younger woman has more reproductive value than an older woman, simply because she has greater life expectancy. Human males universally equate youth with beauty.

In the selection process, some females get left out. Ultimately, in humans as in all animals that copulate, males choose which females reproduce, and male decisions determine female characteristics. The opposite is also true. Females choose which males reproduce, and some males get left out. Females determine male characteristics. This is just the natural order of things. It is what Darwin called sexual selection, but whether by chance or design, it is the way nature is supposed to work. Survival of the fittest is sometimes the same as survival of the prettiest.

What do Women Want?

Women also look for certain physical characteristics. A woman instinctively prefers a man who is able to protect her and her offspring. She looks for a man with good muscle mass, above average height, and an athletic figure. A light step, quick movements, and coordination are desirable. Women like men who can dance or who succeed in sports.

But women's likes are more complicated than that. The peacock is a standard model for male attractiveness. A peacock attracts the attention of the peahens by displaying huge, brilliant tail feathers. Such tails would seem to be detrimental to their owners. They have no intrinsic survival value at all. The tails are large, bulky, and highly visible to predators. They are a hindrance to a peacock that needs to forage in difficult terrain or escape a predator. They also require a huge investment of dietary protein and other nutrients.

The peacock strategy is common among vertebrates. The male is communicating to the peahen that he has resources to waste. He is providing her with visible evidence that his genes are so excellent, and his ability to find food and escape predators is so good, that he can display this ostentatious tail and get away with it. The tail is an example of bravado, of showing off the quality of one's genes.

And the female buys it. She does so because it really is a valid representation of the quality of the male's genes. He does have to be an exceptional survivor in order to produce and maintain such a tail. It is in her best interests to have those genes for her offspring. Also, it is in the best interest of her progeny that her sons have tails like that, so that they will be able to attract peahens, and extend her genes into the next generation. She is genetically programmed to choose the guy who is the biggest showoff. It is survival of the prettiest.

David is a colleague of mine. He is a tall, good-looking professional man who drives a brightly colored sports car. He has been married and divorced twice and is paying child support to four different women. His first live-in girlfriend had a set of twins before they separated. His first wife had a single child by him. His second wife had two children, and his latest girlfriend has a single child by him.

David is like the peacock with the brightest tail feathers. Women flock to him because of his good looks and his high earning power. He has had good reproductive success. He probably has additional offspring that he is not supporting. There is a high likelihood that he has cuckolded other men. He has the genetic material women look for when they roam.

Men are like peacocks in their own way. In primitive societies, they wear the brightest bird feathers they can find, or dive from trees with vines tied around their ankles. In our culture, they drive oversized pick-up trucks or sporty cars. They engage in rowdy, dangerous behavior, make loud noises, and play rough games. Racecar drivers, bull riders, rock musicians, and professional athletes all have their hordes of groupies.

Theresa was a forty-two year old married professional woman visiting from out of town for a conference. She arrived in my ER in a panic just after midnight. She needed a condom removed from her vagina, and she needed post-exposure birth control. That is to say, she needed the "morning after" pill. She was in the company of an embarrassed-looking, twenty-year-old local cowboy.

Here is an example of a woman who gave in to her primitive short-term mating instincts. She sought out an attractive lover for a one-night stand while she was away from her husband and her social network. Unfortunately, things went wrong when the condom slipped off his penis, placing her at risk of both pregnancy and discovery.

Of course, he was also engaged in short-term mating. She was available and he had no reason not to engage in sex with her. However, he did incur some risk. He was ultimately embarrassed by the incident, having to appear in the ER, and having to be identified as the male whose penis was too small for the condom.

When searching for short-term mating opportunities, human females seek out males who advertise the quality of their genes through their expensive toys and dangerous behavior. This is why men do such silly things. They ride bulls, race cars, ride motorcycles, smoke cigarettes, flout authority, and jump off cliffs into shallow water. They do it to impress women. And it works. This is why good girls like bad boys. Rowdy boys are showing off their good genes. They have energy and resources to waste. That is why they are so much more interesting and entertaining than a man who is merely a good, stable provider.

Eric came to my ER with a broken ankle. He was with a group of college students who went on a canoeing trip. They stopped in an area of the river where there are cliffs along one shore. The girls swam in the water or lay in the sun on the opposite shore, while the boys jumped into the water from successively higher cliffs. They kept at it until Eric broke his ankle and had to be taken to the hospital.

This is typical bravado. Boys show off. They do so partly to get the attention of the girls. But even if the girls had not been watching, the boys were watching each other. They were engaged in a competition to determine who could be the most reckless without getting injured. Eric lost.

Often men are trying to impress other men. They know the advantage that is enjoyed by a man who stands out in the crowd, who is admired and respected by other men. Women know that men know which men have the best survival potential. Women look for men who are leaders, men who have power. Political power is universally attractive to women. The captain of the football team is more tempting than one of the linemen. The CEO of a corporation is a better catch than one of the salesmen. The village headman is more attractive than the village cobbler.

The attractiveness of rowdy boys and powerful men is the reason that women sometimes do such silly things. This is why a woman has an affair with her husband's boss, or a married woman has an affair with her married gynecologist. This is why a twenty-year-old White House intern sneaks into a closet with a sixty-year-old man for a little impromptu stand-up sex.

This is also why a woman will sometimes yield much more easily to a proposition from an irresponsible man than to entreaties from a quality male who has potential to be a long-term mate. She sees the former as a short-term mate only, and acts accordingly. However, when the quality man approaches, she will display chastity and play hard to get, trying to exhibit the qualities of a good long-term mate.

Likewise, a man may spend excessive amounts of money on a woman of poor mate potential, anticipating immediate rather than long-term rewards. The same man may behave more frugally and responsibly around a woman who he wishes to woo as the mother of his children. Women know this, and those who consider themselves a long-term investment may refuse gifts they feel are excessive. They are communicating the message that they want a monogamous relationship rather than a fling.

But monogamy has its own costs.

7

The Monogamy Dilemma

All who have meditated on the art of governing mankind have been convinced that the fate of empires depends on the education of youth.

ARISTOTLE

Why does the idea of monogamy persist in society? We humans are not naturally monogamous, and yet we try to convince ourselves that we are. The behavior must provide some advantage to the individuals that practice it. Cultures that encourage monogamy must survive better than promiscuous cultures. However, monogamy has costs, in terms of lost opportunities, personal loneliness, and the efforts expended keeping human instincts in check. It has negative effects on individuals and on society which must be offset by some benefits.

Our natural reproductive behaviors served us well until a few millennia ago. Under primitive conditions, children were raised by their parents for only a few years. Once weaned, a child was raised by the tribe or village, and that was adequate for a primitive culture. The parents moved on to find new mates and make more babies.

This is exactly where my junior colleague Caroline finds herself. She and the father of her child have fallen out of love, and she is searching for a new mate. She is following her genetic programming, doing what feels right to her, even though it violates the rules of her culture. She was taught that she and her husband would stay in love, but her reproductive relationship has followed an entirely different course, one that is actually more consistent with human nature.

While human genetics have changed very little during the past 10,000 years, the social structure of humanity has changed enormously. We are still inclined to pair bond, but the pair bond interval is far too short for the educational needs of a technological culture. Simple pair-bonding has distinct disadvantages in the modern world. The perpetuation of technological cultures requires extended parenting and education. Any culture that can keep parents together beyond the natural pair-bond duration will have an advantage over those that do not. The four-year pair bond may be adequate to assure the survival of the children of Kalahari Bushmen, but it is not enough time to educate the citizens of the Western world. And this is part of the answer to the question I proposed to Caroline. The reason she feels compelled to ignore her instincts and follow the rules of society is that she knows a two-parent upbringing is best for her child and best for the society and culture in which she lives.

Under natural conditions, children drift away from their parents' control shortly after weaning, and are raised by the more general community. All education is informal, coming from older relatives in the village. That education continues throughout life, but children begin sexual activity and become adults at puberty, the biological onset of reproductive capability. That is what our Paleolithic ancestors did. That is the social environment under which early humans thrived. It is what people do who currently live in primitive societies.

As cultures compete with each other for land and resources in an overpopulated world, some survive and some perish. The survival of advanced societies is utterly dependent on investment in many years of childhood education. The society that does the best job of educating its youth dominates other societies, economically and militarily. By extension, the society that keeps parents together to raise their children through college has the advantage over those that raise their children only through kindergarten. Chance of survival is enhanced for both progeny and culture when parents remain devoted to each other and to the raising of their children beyond the natural duration of their pair bond. Ultimately, the most successful culture is the one that best persuades parents to stay together "for the sake of the children." The best way to raise children is in a two-parent home. It maximizes parental investment in their rearing and education. All measures of childhood achievement show that the best parenting is long-term dual parenting. But long-term parenting is not without problems.

The extended parenting of modern civilizations requires that children remain under the supervision and control of their parents long past early childhood. Contact with other adults and older children is tightly controlled by parents. Children are sent to schools, confined on campuses, and made to adhere to artificial schedules. Contact with their peers is rigidly restricted to non-sexual activities. This is all very unnatural. It does not seem fair to adolescents. It does not feel right to them and, not surprisingly, it is resented by them. That is why many teenagers are so rebellious. It is the reason that compliance often requires the strong-handed support of authorities. It is also why some children completely reject the control of their parents, either literally, by running away, or symbolically, through contrarian behavior. Humans are not yet a fully domesticated species.

Adolescents have powerful hormonal drives to leave their parents and find mates of their own. In our modern societies, the restrictions they live under feel wrong and unjust. Human adolescents are not designed to stay at home as long as they do in the modern world. Conflict between adolescents and adults has historically inspired young adults to advance the spread of humanity around the globe by leaving home. Youth emigrates. It reduces inbreeding.

As is often the case, what is difficult for children is even more difficult for their parents. Consider the strain of extended child rearing on the parents, who are well equipped emotionally to raise small children, but are at a loss for skills to control adolescents. The conflict between children and parents in homes containing teenagers is trans-cultural. It is a staple theme in literature in all cultures.

The conflict between children and adults in extended pair bonds, though, is minor compared to the conflict generated between the adult parents. The original pair bond is held together by a selflessness that comes from the collapse of ego boundaries and the merging of egos. Once those ego boundaries re-form, couples are no longer lovers, but ex-lovers. They find themselves obligated, for life, to a home, mortgage, family, and marriage with a relative stranger whom they may or may not like. Keeping them together as faithful couples is a tough task. Monogamy may be best for the children and society, but it is still not what humans are designed to do. It is uncomfortable for humans to extend the pair bond beyond its natural length. As the bond wanes, couples cease loving each other, and often cease liking each other as well. Their mutual lust vanishes. The woman tires of giving sex to a man she doesn't like, and the man tires of paying bills for a woman he doesn't like. No matter how strong their genuine friendship used to be, they eventually become embittered about their relationship, not understanding how it came to be this way. They do not understand that this is the natural course of a relationship because they do not understand the nature of the original pair bond. Such embitterment ruins relationships between people who often started out as good friends. They accumulate anger and resentment, and it interferes with their companionship.

Perhaps this is why so many couples become better friends after they divorce. According to Constance Ahrons, in *The Good Divorce*, about fifteen percent of divorced couples return to being good friends. Another thirty-five percent remain on relatively good terms and co-parent their children with minimal conflict. Her studies show that half of divorced couples get along better after the divorce than they did before. Once they abandon the unrealistic expectations associated with the original pair bond, they can go back to being friends again.

After the pair bond expires, the couple are no longer lovers, but rather ex-lovers.

Yet each of them remains totally dependent on the other to meet their emotional, economic, personal, and sexual needs. They are forbidden from seeking solace from outside the marriage. But each becomes increasingly disinterested in meeting the needs of the other. They find themselves trapped in limbo, unable to obtain the intimacy and affection they need from their spouses, and yet prohibited from seeking it elsewhere. They accumulate anger and resentment over their unmet needs. Quarrelling ensues. Their injured feelings drive a wedge between them. They become isolated and emotionally disengaged, and begin seeking their emotional support and affection from others. This is, after all, what they are genetically programmed to do.

Now, the ex-lovers must make choices about engaging in infidelity. When a pair bond ends, the natural human inclination is to start looking for a new mate. Although straying is prohibited by marriage vows, people are genetically programmed to follow their instincts. But they feel guilty for showing interest in people other than their spouses, and they become angry when spouses have the "wandering eye." They accumulate resentment over broken promises made during the early stages of the pair bond, failing to recognize that such promises are ephemeral. They equate infidelity with betrayal and rejection. And, yet, if they do not stray, they feel regret over their lost opportunities. They find themselves surrounded by other unhappy, lonely humans who are in outdated pairs, or are unpaired, but they are obligated to keep all relationships outside their marriage non-romantic. This is often an insurmountable challenge. Humans are still genetically Paleolithic, and they often find themselves in a world of relationships for which they are poorly adapted, permanently paired with someone they no longer love, while restricted from reaching out to potential new lovers.

If you fear loneliness, then do not marry.

Chekov

Infidelity can introduce more than just conflict into a marriage. It can undermine the whole purpose of monogamy by introducing questions of paternity. Uncertain paternity is the bane of extended parental investment. Fidelity was not so important when humans were ignorant of paternity, and relationships were brief, and new mates were just around the corner. However, when there is only one brood of offspring per lifetime, few men are willing to invest heavily in the future of children who may not be theirs. It is a rare man who willingly pays for twenty years of food, lodging, clothing, auto insurance, and private school tuition for another man's children.

Maintaining an exhausted pair bond is difficult enough without all this bitterness. It is hard to provide support and services to each other when the desire to do so is gone. The additional burden of guilt and recrimination makes the task all but impossible. Couples come to feel that they are in constant conflict with one another when, in fact, the real conflict is between their biological programming and their social obligations. Primitive instincts compel them to do things that they know are not in the best interests of their children or their society. In advanced cultures, people really do stay together as couples for the sake of the children, but also for the benefit to themselves and their society. Staying together for the children is not a failure of the relationship. It is a maturing of the original pair bond into a long-term post-romantic relationship.

Traditional Judeo-Christian marriage is an indefinite extension of the pair bond well into the post-romantic phase, and it places a great burden upon a married couple. They must continue to behave as if they are pair-bonded when they are not. This is why so many couples feel that their marriage is a sham. They are only pretending to be in love.

The extended relationship will be made easier if couples understand that it is normal for lovers to lose interest when the pair bond matures. They must understand that they share with each other many of the same sacrifices and discomforts, and that these are simply the result of human nature. They should help each other overcome the loneliness, sadness, and regrets that are intrinsic to the extended rearing of children in a modern society. They can do this by being understanding of each other's feelings, and by actively working to provide for each other's needs, even after their natural inclination to do so has diminished. They must transition to a new form of partnership based less on romance, and more on friendship. It may help if each of them takes a few minutes each day to recall why they fell in love in the first place.

8

Making Monogamy Work

It is not a lack of love,
but a lack of friendship
that makes unhappy marriages.

FRIEDRICH NIETZSCHE

As a philosophy, monogamy has served humans well by providing extended rearing for children. But it conflicts with human instincts and creates problems that could be avoided. The belief that humans are naturally monogamous is destructive for two reasons. First, when romance fades unexpectedly, it leads to the shame, guilt, and resentment that destroys relationships. Second, it implies that relationships spontaneously hold themselves together, when, in fact, they do not. Cementing a post-romantic relationship requires a plan and an understanding of the differences between the romantic and post-romantic bonds.

Many marriages do last for a lifetime. There are emotional forces that can bind together a post-romantic relationship for half a century or more. There is continued value in an exhausted pair bond. There is something in the repertoire of human instincts and emotions that can hold together post-romantic relationships. Durable, long-lasting partnerships are made up not of passion, but of mutualism, respect, and reciprocity. Passion may be desirable in the short-term, but it does not hold up in the long-term.

As romance fades in a relationship, it becomes less of a love affair and more of a social partnership. All long-term partnerships have certain things in common. They are held together by basic human instincts that are not directly related to breeding. Such instincts are present in romantic relation-ships as well, but are completely overshadowed by the blind-ing passion of romance. Post-romantic couples, and, for that matter, all non-romantic human relationships extending all the way up to international politics, are held together by altruism, reciprocity, empathy, shared kin, complementarity, and shared goals. Additionally, they are inhibited from dis-solution by inactivity inertia, fear of loss, fear of loneliness, and fear of retribution. They are further impacted by exter-nal social forces arising from religious beliefs, family expecta-tions, and financial, legal, and moral obligations.

The Binding Forces of Long-Term Relationships

Reciprocal altruism is the inclination to provide services to another without any expectation of immediate reward, but with the understanding that an eventual reciprocal service will occur. This is not unique to humans; it has been well documented in non-human primates. Reciprocal altruism is simple back-scratching. It is plain old-fashioned fairness. Successful couples help each other meet their separate goals. They support each other, provide for each other, and recipro-cate each other's efforts toward the relationship. Couples take turns putting each other through college. They provide for each other's personal needs. They support each other through emotional crises, and stroke each other's egos. They do the dishes out of turn for each other. They do nice things for each other. They continue to invest of themselves in each other's welfare.

Reciprocal altruism extends beyond goal-oriented behaviors, though. It is a philosophy about how members of a couple should treat each other. It is the basis of all the advice given in so many relationship books about mutual respect, honesty, politeness, tolerance, and forgiveness. It is the Golden Rule and the basis of good friendship.

People will put up with all kinds of emotional insults and unfairness during the heat of passion, sacrificing a certain amount of their self-respect for the sake of the relationship. They are betting that what they gain from the relationship will eventually cover their losses. Once the opportunity to breed has passed, though, and the initial passion is gone, the prospects for the future of a relationship are much less promising. Ex-lovers are much less forgiving of trespasses. Failure to adhere to the principles of reciprocal altruism in a post-romantic relationship drives a partner away.

Mature relationships survive best when people treat their partners as they would like to be treated. Reciprocity means that each party to the relationship is fair to the other, each performing their duties and accepting their fair share of the work of living together. They are truthful to one another in their words, body language, and actions. They are tolerant of what they see as faults in each other. They do not hold each other responsible for things beyond their control. They do not become angry at each other for being who they are, for expressing their basic human nature. They forgive each other's genuinely regretted misbehaviors, and accept each other's sincere apologies. When they fight, they fight fairly.

Kin altruism is the inclination to provide services that benefit one's relatives with no reward to one's self. The only benefit accrued by the individual is the increase in his or her family genes in the population. This is the basis of the social behaviors of ants, termites, and bees. The workers are all sisters. Only the queen lays eggs and produces young, while all the work of caring for the young is done by their older sisters, who forego the opportunity to lay eggs of their own. Kin altruism is the very heart of parenting. It is the reason that parents, aunts, uncles, and grandparents dote on children.

But it is also important in selecting and caring for a mate. Humans generally choose mates who resemble the people they grew up with. It is a basic instinct. Men tend to choose women who are like their mothers in mannerisms, language, dress, and culture. Likewise, women tend to choose men who are like their fathers. People are more comfortable around people who resemble their relatives. People choose their mates from their own society, culture, and community.

Kin altruism is the glue that holds together social networks. A social network is the entire body of social contacts that an individual possesses. It is the accumulated mass of a person's acquaintances, and their interrelationships. Social networks are generally composed of persons who are of the same, or at least similar, cultures. When two people come together to form a couple, they are not isolated individuals. They have social networks, which also merge, and which must also be compatible.

People are more inclined to trust, help, empathize with, provide comfort and care for, ask directions from, and give directions to people who look and act like themselves. They are more comfortable interacting with people who dress like them, speak their language, and have their facial features and skin color. They are more inclined to enter into arrangements of trust with someone who looks familiar, rather than with someone who looks unfamiliar, whether it involves dating, pair-bonding, marriage, business contracts, or apartment leases.

Empathy is the ability of one person to observe the actions of another and infer the emotions of that individual, then experience those emotions personally. People feel sad when seeing someone else be sad. They feel the suffering, humiliation, anger, and emotional pain of others. They also feel the joy, happiness, and relief of others. This is what makes it possible for Hollywood and Disney to work their magic. When humans observe actors or cartoon images on a screen, they can relate to the emotions of the characters.

Empathy also makes relationships work. Empathetic persons are aware of the feelings of others, and take this into account when interacting with a spouse. They try to avoid hurting each other's feelings. Empathetic persons will expend their efforts to reduce the suffering of another in order to reduce their own discomfort. When people cry, others try to help because the crying makes them sad. People try to make others happy, so that they can feel happy themselves. When a woman cries because of her partner's actions, the partner may become sad, and may back-peddle on his position. When a man is upset over something his partner has said or done, she becomes sad and may alter her behavior.

Shared goals bond couples. The sharing of goals is different from reciprocal altruism. Altruism involves one person expending efforts toward the goal of another person, while a shared goal means that people are working on the same thing together. Joint efforts toward common goals--whether it entails building a new house or just getting through the chores of another day--bind people together. The most important goal shared by a set of parents is the raising of their mutual offspring. In fact, it is the purpose most often given for preserving a marriage in the absence of a loving relationship. Couples stay together for the sake of the children.

Couples share meals, hobbies, retirement goals, travel plans, houses, gardens, libraries, professional interests, woodworking projects, vacations, favorite foods, and favorite movies. They share good habits and bad habits. They share good times and disasters. They share friends and enemies. They share chores and joys. They share their experiences during the day, and their emotions about the day. They share their time with each other. Parents also share the raising of their children. They share the goal of getting their children ready for independent life as adults. And they hope to share the spoiling of their grandchildren. This is companionship, and it is the life-blood of human relationships.

Complementarity means that people work together best when each of them can cover for the shortcomings of the other. Humans naturally tend to choose mates who have some skills and talents that complement their own. That is, each member of the pair has abilities that the other lacks. Complementarity strengthens a relationship. It may do so, in part, by providing ample opportunities for reciprocal altruism. Or, each person may come to rely on the other for certain functions, and after time, they become so dependent on one another that they form a single functional unit. They are able to accomplish more together, and are more financially stable, and, therefore, under less stress, when they have a high degree of complementarity.

This is reminiscent of the Chinese concept of Yin and Yang, the great duality of nature, in which two complementary parts form a whole. It is the Jewish concept of man and woman being two half-souls who form one complete soul when combined in marriage. It is the Christian ideal of two souls intertwined, two hearts that beat as one, bound together in a union ordained by God.

Religion is a relative newcomer to marriage. The institution of marriage preceded contemporary religion by many thousands of years. Spiritual components of marital relationships emerged gradually over the past two millennia, and now play a dominant role in binding together post-romantic couples. Judeo-Christian religions teach that falling in love and forming a pair bond identifies two people who God created as soul mates. This creates a huge conceptual threshold that must be overcome before a Judeo-Christian can abandon a relationship. One member of the couple must first invalidate the original pair bond by convincing herself that the original act of falling in love was not real, and that her partner was misidentified as her one true love. The defector will convince herself that it must not have been true love, but just lust or infatuation.

Religion is an important joint effort for any couple, and is a major factor in the selection of a mate. Many people define their sense of purpose and their life goals based upon their religious beliefs. These are powerful concepts to share. People who are of the same religion will undoubtedly share a great many other things. They share the same afterlife for eternity. They share a huge portion of their social networks. Religious congruity is a powerful positive stabilizing force in post-romantic relationships.

Religion binds couples through negative forces, too. Social costs are levied against parties when they break the bonds of matrimony. Religious couples may stay in relationships to avoid both the spiritual and the social consequences of defection. Abandoning a relationship may result in being shunned by one's religious community. This, in turn, results in the loss of a large part of one's social network, including kin contacts, business associates, and potential alternative mates. Some religions additionally impose social restrictions or penalties on people who leave sanctioned marriages, and these can be quite severe. Religious authorities can impose humiliation, banishment, death, and eternal damnation on those who leave a spouse or betray a sanctioned marriage through adultery or abandonment.

Civil authorities, likewise, place restrictions on the dissolution of the relationships they have sanctioned. The financial cost of divorce can be a significant barrier to couples, and many people end up separating without formal legal proceedings. In Western cultures, punitive measures are generally restricted to matters of support payments and child custody arrangements, which make it more difficult for the man to leave a marriage. Legal expenditures can be prohibitory in cultures where attorneys are allowed to antagonize the divorcing parties.

In the Muslim cultures and some other strongly patriarchal Eastern and African societies the laws are more punitive to women than to men. A woman who leaves a marriage may be forced to pay large sums of money to her husband or his family. A woman who abandons her husband and takes up with another man may be imprisoned or even executed for adultery.

Inactivity Inertia requires some explanation. The strongest forces binding relationships are internal, and the most ubiquitous of these is inactivity inertia. This concept is best illustrated by a small sea creature called a limpet, a type of mollusk, a seashell. Limpets live on rocks between the high and low tide lines on rocky seashores. They are referred to as sessile creatures. That is to say, they do not move much. They are grazers and generally roam only small distances from their home locations on rocks on the shoreline, always returning to their personal crevices every day. For many years, the question of whether limpets could move to a new home remained unanswered. Naturalists who study such things painted numbers on limpet shells, and drew lines around them on the rocks, and photographed their rocky abodes month after month, and tried all sorts of experiments to answer this fundamental question of nature. What the naturalists eventually determined is that limpets can move to a new home, but they generally don't. They just stay where they are.

The world is a dangerous place for limpets. If they get too close to the bottom of a rock, passing seabirds can stand on the sand at low tide and pry them off. If they get too low in the water, they are not exposed at low tide, and starfish will prey on them. If they get too high on the rock, they will not be covered at high tide, and they will dry out, or sea birds can stand on top of the rocks and reach over the edge and pry them off.

Limpets cannot see or hear. They cannot stand up and look off into the distance. They cannot know what conditions will be like anywhere except where they are. They have no way of determining how safe another place might be, or how far it may be to safety, or how much danger is in their immediate vicinity, or how hazardous a journey might be. All in all, if you are a limpet, and you are alive where you are, no matter how bad your local situation may be, your best bet is to just stay there. For a limpet, the greatest safety is in inactivity.

People are a lot like limpets. They tend to stay where they are, even when things might be better elsewhere. The reliability of their information about elsewhere is not as good as it is for their present location. The act of moving is dangerous and expensive in itself. Unless the current situation is very bad, or the promise of a new situation is very good, the move is not justified. There is an inertial threshold that must be overcome before people will activate change.

Inactivity inertia is one of the things that compel people to stay in bad relationships. This is why a woman stays with an ill-tempered, abusive, lazy husband or a man stays with a selfish, unloving, overspending wife. It is why nations keep bad governments and people stay in bad jobs. It is also why people who have been in their jobs for a long time are typically paid less than new hires in the same position. Business savvy employers know just how much they can underpay their loyal veteran workers. They know that veteran employees are limpets who will not leave until the pay elsewhere is a great deal higher. Likewise, abusive people have a sense for how much they can mistreat their spouses before they exceed the threshold for desertion.

Fear of retribution is a barrier that keeps couples together by preventing one or the other from leaving. Some people become abusive or punitive at any suggestion of disloyalty by a spouse. Like the male baboons that bite and strike their harem females who wander too far, some humans mistreat their spouses if they suspect any inclination toward infidelity or desertion. A man typically threatens physical abuse, while the woman threatens financial revenge through attorneys. In extreme cases, one parent may mentally or physically abuse or even kill the children.

Fear of loss and loneliness can keep people together long after love is gone. They fear losing their home, children, and in-laws. They fear losing their self-respect, their social station, and their social networks. They fear losing the investment they have made in their partner, and the companionship they obtain even from a bad spouse. Companionship and escape from loneliness are powerful driving forces that cannot be ignored.

Humans have a deeply rooted need for companionship, ranking right up there with food and water. No matter what incompatibilities two people may have, when they are both lonely, they have a lot in common. Some people stay in relationships simply because they are afraid they will have no one else to be with. They stay because they have invested themselves in the relationship up to that point, and will lose that investment. For most humans, no matter how emotionally impoverished a relationship may be, it is better than being alone. People fear the absence of companionship. Most humans cannot survive as solitary creatures.

Summary

Post-romantic relationships can persist in good health for decades, maintained by a combination of forces, positive and negative, internal and external. The positive forces are reciprocal altruism, kin altruism, empathy, sharing of goals, and sharing of social networks. The negative forces are inactivity inertia, fear of the unknown, avoidance of loss of companionship and investment, fear of retribution, and avoidance of loneliness. External pressures come from civil authorities, and assert primarily negative forces. They apply penalties for dissolution of the relationship. Religion exerts powerful positive forces, through provision of moral structures and social networks, and also exerts negative pressures, through punitive responses to adultery and desertion.

Every relationship is a unique combination of human interactions. Relationships are as varied as the human beings who form them. Generally, a good relationship is one that is held together primarily by positive forces. A bad relationship is one that is dominated by negative forces. Unfortunately, it is not often clear where a given relationship falls. Any relationship that is held together by consistently great sex and perfectly compatible social networks is clearly good. Any relationship that is held together by mutual drug dependency, shared homelessness, reciprocal abuse, and fear of retribution is clearly bad.

But most relationships depend on a combination of positive and negative forces. They shift back and forth, having good times and bad times. That is encouraging. It means that most troubled relationships can be improved easily. They can be nudged over to the good side, often with surprisingly little effort. It just takes a basic understanding of the principles involved and a willingness to apply them. A great wealth of advice can be found in the "Relationships" section of any bookstore. The underlying principles are simple, but they are impossible to implement in the setting of shame, guilt, and resentment that often dominates a failing relationship. If people understand why the pair bond ended, why they fell out of love, and why their ego-boundaries came back up, then this advice is much easier to take. And here, in condensed form, is what those relationship books say.

To Sustain the Relationship

As the romance fades in a pair bond, you and your partner should cultivate a friendship that will maintain your relationship for the rest of your lives. The first step in this process is to refrain from being angry about the fading romance. Do not get caught up in the turmoil of guilt, shame, and resentment that can so easily destroy a friendship. Remember that it is normal for the pair bond to end. Relationships change over time. You are not by nature a monogamous creature, and neither is your spouse.

You and your partner should merge your social networks or create a shared social network. Many couples isolate themselves from their social networks during their pair bond, and re-emerge as the pair bond starts to wane. They then find themselves in separate circles of friends and growing apart. Construction of the shared social network should start early so that the couple has a shared circle of friends to hold them together.

Find common interests and goals. The foremost of these is the children of the marriage. Others can be art, the home, the garden, music, square dancing, mountain climbing, karaoke, kiting, kayaking, or kangaroo hunting. It doesn't matter. Just find something the two of you like to do and get used to doing it together.

Support each other's goals. Each member of a couple has his own dreams and aspirations. Each has something he needs to do on his own. It may be the completion of an education, the opening of a toy store, or the construction of a perfect chess board. It doesn't matter. Just identify what your partner dreams of, and help him achieve it. Invest yourself in the dreams of your partner.

As the romance fades, have faith in yourself and in your spouse. The two of you were once fused into one entity by a pair bond, and you believed that you could overcome all difficulties together. The original pair bond may be gone, but the two of you are still who you were then. Together you can overcome great adversities, even those that come from within.

Be nice to your spouse. Be polite and kind at all times. Treat your spouse with all the respect and kindness deserving of the single most important person to you out of all the six billion people on Earth.

Touch your spouse often and encourage your spouse to touch you. Enjoy closeness. Remember that you are the only source of intimate physical affection allowed to your spouse. Remember the opportunities your spouse sacrifices in order to be with you. Continue to court and to actively love your spouse.

Be truthful to yourself and your spouse. Think before you speak. Be sure that you are saying what you believe to be true. Express your truth clearly. Avoid ambiguity and mixed messages. Remember the promises you made to your spouse when you fell in love. They are still binding.

Do your share of the work in all the different components of the relationship. This does not just mean housework. It means working the same number of hours in a day, whether those hours are spent in child-rearing, housekeeping, or on the job. It means graciously accepting your share of the pain, drudgery, and hardship. It also means sharing the compromises equally, carrying your share of the burden of submission, of yielding to your partner, of biting your tongue and agreeing.

Complain when you need to, criticize only if you must, but do not be contemptuous or condescending. Do not say or do things in a manner intended only to hurt feelings and damage your mate's self-esteem. Your communication should convey information, not inflict injury. Behave at all times as if your spouse is a lifetime companion and a lifelong investment.

There is one more concept that is essential to understanding the dynamics of transitioning relationships. A person does not need to be nice to a lover in the heat of a love affair. Someone who is madly in love will tolerate all kinds of abusive behavior from a partner. The love will last longer if the rules above are followed, but it will persist for a while even if they are not. However, the rules above become absolute in the post-romantic relationship. In other words, you don't have to be nice to someone who loves you. They will stay anyway, just because they love you. However, you do have to be nice to people who do not love you, or they will just leave. This means that in order for a relationship to persist, as the relationship matures, as time goes on, you have to be nicer and nicer to your partner.

From Post-Romantic to Post-Marital

If all this fails, then consider that you and your spouse simply do not share enough in common to fill a lifetime together, or you do not have enough complementarity to survive as a couple, or you have social networks that are just too incompatible. This sometimes happens when two people marry for love. If it does, then recognize and accept it. Do not blame your spouse or yourself. People know a great deal more about each other after four years of marriage than they did when they first fell in love. The two of you got into this situation together, and you should help each other get out safely. Do not burden yourself or your spouse with guilt, shame, and resentment. Do not become angry or vengeful. Instead, approach a separation following the same principles outlined above.

After all, divorce does not end a relationship. It changes it to a new kind of relationship. The two of you took vows that contained promises, and those promises bind you for the rest of your lives. You cannot erase your personal histories. You are the total of your life experiences, and you cannot change that. You and your spouse have social responsibilities to each other that extend beyond the end of the marriage. You may no longer share a bed, but you still share the same world. You may continue to share the same social network. You will certainly share your children, and, hopefully, you will share your grandchildren.

So, if you do choose to separate, do it graciously and politely. Help each other through the process. Work together to form a new, post-marital relationship that continues to provide for the needs of yourselves and your children. Help each other get on with new lives.

Remember, incredible as it may seem, this is what humans do under natural conditions. Humans are instinctively programmed to separate after a few years and go on to find new mates. It should not be surprising that so many marriages fail to last a lifetime. Rather, it should be surprising that so many last as long as they do. It is sad that so many couples are led to believe that they have personally failed when they stop loving each other. They become entangled in emotional turmoil and drama. Their shame, guilt, and resentment prevent them from working together constructively. They fail to gain insight into the causes of their animosity, leaving them doomed to repeat their mistakes in the next relationship.

A great deal of human suffering will be avoided if young people are taught that they are not truly designed to stay together as life-long couples. There are good reasons for them to try to stay together, but it is not natural. We humans are genetically programmed to leave behind a trail of ex-lovers, and to remain on good terms with them, living in the same village or forest, sharing the raising of children, and continuing to respect and care for each other long after our pair bonds end. Remember, the whole point of the process was, and for the most part still is, to raise healthy children who can populate the next generation. Any pair bond that results in a new crop of well-adjusted adults is a biological success, whether it lasts for four years or forty.

My good friend Katlyn is a wonderful example. She divorced a few years ago, and lamented to me how ashamed and embarrassed she felt over the failure of her marriage. She and her husband were married twenty-three years, and raised two sons, who both completed undergraduate college degrees.

I counseled her that she was being unfairly critical of herself and of her husband. The two of them have raised their children well. They have completed an entirely successful marriage. They should congratulate each other over a bottle of champagne and celebrate their achievement. And they should feel free to separate and find love again with whomever they wish. If they can discard their shame, guilt, and resentment, they may even find love again with each other.

Kissing don't last, cookery do.

George Meredith

9

Marriage: Social Bonding

And a man shall leave his mother
And a woman leave her home
And they shall travel on to where
The two shall be as one.

THE WEDDING SONG, BY NOEL "PAUL" STOOKEY

Here are some Western definitions of marriage:

New Webster's Dictionary 1993: "The institution under which a man and a woman become legally united on a permanent basis." Short and simple.

Oxford English Dictionary: "The condition of being husband and wife. The relationship between married persons. Spouse hood. Wedlock." .... followed by a 3,600 word discourse on etymology and variations.

> *Wikipedia.com, 2009*: "Marriage is a social, spiritual, and/or legal union of individuals. ... an institution in which interpersonal relationships (usually intimate and sexual) are acknowledged by the state, by religious authority, or by both." Note the absence of gender and number.

What is this thing called marriage? It is a ubiquitous behavior among humans. Some form of marriage is recognized in every culture, no matter how primitive or advanced, but the configuration is astoundingly variable. It ranges from the most informal, personal, private declarations to internationally witnessed and sanctioned events binding together the fortunes of great nations and huge populations. It may be accepted to last only as long as the couple wish, or be mandated to last until the end of not only their lives, but also the lives of their descendants. It can be a simple agreement between two lovers, or it may involve their families, their communities, local political entities, religious authorities, sovereign states, and international immigration boards. It may impose absolute sexual exclusivity, or be completely "open," or anywhere in between. The two parties may be intimate lovers or complete strangers. Some marriages do not include any arrangement for sexual activity at all, and some married couples never meet.

People tend to have a narrow view of marriage, thinking that the term means only the legal arrangement that is common in their own society. For the industrialized Western world, this generally means that marriage is between two people, a man and a woman, and it occurs when they fall in love and decide to raise a family. However, in the overall theater of humanity, most marriages are between two people who are not in love, and the majority of couples who fall in love do not marry, and the majority of children are not raised within the shelter of a marriage. In fact, many marriages are not confined to one man and one woman, and many do not include both sexes in the union.

In the United States, where the law sanctions typical Judeo-Christian marriage traditions, the 2006 National Vital Statistics Report reveals that thirty-eight percent of children are born out of wedlock. This is up from thirty-two percent in 1996 and twenty-three percent in 1986. The increase is primarily among women in their twenties and thirties who have chosen to be single mothers, rather than among teenagers, who presumably just don't know any better. It may be that more women are choosing single motherhood simply because the new liberal sexuality makes it so difficult for a woman to recruit a traditional husband. Worldwide, the rate of out-of-wedlock birth is about twenty-five percent, based on figures compiled in the late 1990s. When these figures are added to the divorce rates for couples with children, more than half of the world's children have single parents or stepparents.

The great majority of the births to unwed mothers are the product of loving relationships that did not advance to marriage. Humans fall in love many more times than they marry. Marriage is no longer required or expected for the parents of a child. Also, marriage is no longer an expected outcome of the process of falling in love. The great majority of human pair bonds end before marriage occurs. Generally, people need more reason to marry than just falling in love or having a child.

I have a young colleague named Dan who was head over heels in love with one of his classmates, Alicia, in their senior year in college. They lived together all through graduate school, but did not marry. During their forth year together, as they approached graduation in their professions, they began to quarrel about their final professional destinations. This issue divided them, and they went their separate ways.

The love affair between Dan and Alicia illustrates the pair-bonding duration. Their pair bond lasted four years and ended over an issue that would have been insignificant in the first year of their relationship. Their ego boundaries had returned and these two people no longer wanted each other enough to sacrifice their individual professional aspirations for the sake of their relationship.

This case also illustrates the importance of extrinsic factors in marriage. These two people were very much in love. They were intensely pair-bonded. But they were not at the correct time and place in their lives for marriage. They put it off too long, and the opportunity expired.

Of course, marriage does not need to be based on love at all. There are still cultures in the modern world that arrange marriages between children or adults who may never have met. There are couples being married today that were introduced on this day, their wedding day. It is very likely that this will occur somewhere in the world on the day that you read this paragraph. And these two complete strangers will be expected to have sex on their wedding night, sometimes with their in-laws there to watch, to witness and confirm that the marriage is consummated! Just feel the love in that relationship!

Furthermore, not all persons in love are entitled to marry. Consider the controversy in the United States over gay marriage. The concept requires a major revision of the moral and legal codes of the prudish and, frankly, provincial Americans. Marriage is defined in the modern Western culture as a union between one man and one woman, but that is a local tradition only. There is a wider tradition of marriage, which is trans-cultural and historical, and which has recognized marriage variously as a union of: one man and one woman; one man and several women; one woman and several men; several men and several women; one man and one tree; one woman and several women; two women; two men; one woman and one deity; one man and one deity; and etc. The point is that restricting the definition of marriage to only one of these arrangements has no anthropological basis. It is purely a matter of cultural preferences, sort of a local option, usually based on religion.

Some Variations on Marriage

1. One man and one woman - Sexually exclusive: This is the standard Judeo-Christian marriage. It first appeared in the fourth century in Christian Europe (Lewis, 2009), and became the norm by the tenth century. It is now common in all modern cultures, where it goes by the name of monogamy.
2. One man and one woman – Not sexually exclusive: Primitive hunter-gatherers and prehistoric people formed pair bonds, but accepted infidelity (Ryan, 2010). This type of marriage persists in many aboriginal cultures (Fielding, 1942). In modern society, it is known as an "open relationship" or "open dyad." In the extreme, it is polyamory. (See below.)
3. One man and several women – Polygynous marriage, such as the harem, was common throughout history, and is still practiced in the Muslim religion and in many primitive cultures (Tonkinson, 1991; Lee, 1993; van den Berghe, 1990).
4. One woman and several men – This is polyandrous marriage, and is traditional in Nepal and Northern India, usually in the form of fraternal polyandry, when several brothers share one wife (Fielding, 1942; van den Berghe, 1990).
5. One woman and several women – Among the American Plains Indians, some women became warriors and took one or more wives (Ewers, 1961, pp 185-190).
6. Several men and several women – In some aboriginal cultures, groups of adults are married, such as a group of brothers in one family to a group of sisters in another, and it is known as group marriage (van der Berghe, 1990). In the modern world, this type of relationship is known as polyamory. Many resources for polyamory can be found on the Internet (polyamory. org; polyamory.com; polyamorysociety.org).

7. One woman and one tree – This is a Hindu custom allowing a woman to escape a common type of astrological curse. (Sundarum, 2007.)

8. One man and one tree – This is also a Hindu marriage tradition related to the belief that an older brother should marry first. When a young man wants to marry, but his older brother is unmarried, the older brother may be married to a tree. This clears the way for the younger brother to marry a woman (Fielding, 1942).

9. Two women (or two men) - Same-sex marriage is currently controversial in the United States, but is accepted in many nations and cultures. Historically, same-sex marriage has been documented for eons. See (Hinsch, 1990, and Boswell, 1995) for examples in ancient Rome and China.

10. One man and one deity - Ancient Sumerian kings married female deities, as did some Celtic kings.

11. One woman and one deity - Catholic nuns in some orders, such as the Franciscan Sisters, are married to Christ (www.torsisters.com/faq.htm).

12. Marriage without sex – This is known as a spiritual marriage or a Josephite marriage in the Catholic church.

13. Arranged marriage – Common throughout the world in both modern and ancient cultures, especially for children (Tonkinson, 1991; van den Berghe, 1990). Even today, the great majority of Hindu marriages are arranged by family members. (Hawley, 2007, pp. 63-75.)

14. Child marriage – Historically, children have been the subject of betrothals in every conceivable combination. Children are not only betrothed to other children, but also to adults (Tonkinson, 1991; van den Berghe, 1990). In some extreme cultures, unborn females were wed to adult males (Fielding, 1942; Janssen, 2002). Child marriages have now been illegalized in the Western world and much of Asia, but still occur in India and Australasia.

Love is recognized in nearly every human culture, but it is not always relevant to marriage. In Western societies, most people who marry are in love, but that was not true for several thousands of years of human history. Even today, love is rarely sufficient cause for two people to wed. There are many other considerations, as in the case of Dan and Alicia. Two people who marry must be at the right time and place in both of their lives. They must have cleared their playing fields of other potential or former mates. They must have the financial ability and legal freedom to marry. Their social networks should be compatible and encouraging of marriage. And, generally, there will be one or several incentives from the list in Table 1 that contribute to their decision.

The Pre-Human History of Marriage

The history of marriage as a behavior begins with the non-human primates, who share some interesting design features with humans. The sexual and interpersonal relationships of gorillas, baboons, chimpanzees, and bonobos demonstrate some surprisingly human attributes.

Gorillas live in groups that include one dominant male and two to seven females, along with their juvenile offspring. They may also take in orphaned juveniles. The male and female bond for life. The females and young stay close to the dominant male, and rely on him for protection from predators and free-roaming male gorillas. The dominant males are highly protective of their females and the juveniles that they have sired, but male gorillas may sometimes kill juveniles that are not their offspring.

Adolescent males and females leave the troop to find mates. A female may join another group, or a male and two or more females may form a new group. The females have a twenty-eight-day menstrual cycle. Females initiate sexual activity when they are in estrus. Males do not initiate sex.

Table 1. Reasons for marriage

Related to child rearing
>   Creating an extended pair bond for the purpose of raising children
>   Formation of a legal family unit
>   Securing a sexual partner for procreation
>   Social stabilization for children born out of wedlock to a couple
>   Procurement of a mother/father for children of a single man/woman
>   Procurement of a provider for children of a single parent
>   Meeting requirements for adoption of children
>   Meeting moral/religious/ethical obligations for an unintended pregnancy

Relating to sex
>   Securing a sexual partner, not for procreation
>   Legitimizing sexual relations with an existing partner

Related to intra-sex competition
>   Finalizing the outcome of competition for a mate
>   Securing a trophy spouse
>   Establishing a legal barrier against adversaries for a sexual partner

Related to property holdings
>   Obtaining pension benefits
>   Securing an inheritance or other property
>   Securing control of property or business that is not owned
>   Merging personal property to improve lifestyle

Related to legal benefits
>   Improving military benefits
>   Avoiding military deployment
>   Obtaining medical insurance coverage
>   Obtaining citizenship

Securing residency other than citizenship
Securing or obtaining social security benefits
Reducing taxes
Meeting qualifications for a mortgage or other housing
Related to public persona
As a public declaration of love
As a public declaration of heterosexuality
As a public declaration of homosexuality
As a publicity stunt
As a public declaration of "normalcy"
Related to social standing
Merging political interests of different families
Social climbing
Fulfilling religious obligations
Related to personal safety
Shotgun weddings
Procurement of protection for a woman and her children
Related to personal loss
Filling the void left by the loss of a spouse
Filling the void left by the loss of a parent
Related to scripting
Meeting perceived parental or community expectations
Following the example set by older siblings

Baboons live in large troops of up to several hundred individuals. A group will typically consist of a number of dominant males, each of which will have a harem of up to five females. These males will jealously guard over their females, and will mistreat them if they stray too far. They will bite and strike females who wander too close to another male.

However, a separate mating strategy exists among baboons, in which a single male and female form a special bond, and stay on the periphery of the troop. This male will help his female find food, and will share his food with any infant in her care. He will defend her and the infant from other males, and from predators. When she is in estrus, she will exclusively mate with him. In the animal behavior literature, the baboons that form these pairs are called "special friends," but their relationship is clearly a primitive romance.

Chimpanzees live in troops of 50 to 150, and are highly promiscuous. The female has a thirty-six-day menstrual cycle. During estrus, her rump becomes red and swollen, advertising her availability to all adult males. At this time, the males may actually line up to copulate with her. Interestingly, males and females who are closely related will not copulate. However, the family structure is matrilineal. That is, the chimps know who their mothers are, but in such a promiscuous society, they cannot know who their fathers are. A female chimp will not mate with her son or brother, but she will very likely copulate with her father, just by chance, because she does not know his identity and she is likely to copulate with every male in the group at some time.

Chimps are highly territorial, and a single animal or small group that wanders into a neighboring territory will almost certainly be killed. However, a female in estrus uses her swollen rump like a passport, and can migrate freely to another group or territory. Her willingness to submit to sex redirects the aggressive energy of males.

Like baboons, chimps sometimes have special friends. Occasionally, a single male and female will leave the troop for a time. They will go off in the jungle by themselves, foraging and grooming, for up to three months. This male will have a monopoly on the female when she is in estrus. Unlike the special friendship of the baboon pair, the incipient romance of the chimps ends once the female becomes pregnant.

Bonobos, also called pigmy chimpanzees, are the most promiscuous of the primates. These creatures have sex constantly, all day long. They have sex as a greeting or when they share food. They use sex to establish rank, sooth hurt feelings, mend relationships, and resolve conflicts. Both the males and females masturbate frequently. There is no bonding between individual adults for reproduction.

Sex among bonobos seems totally unrestricted. It is as common among juveniles as it is among adults. Both males and females initiate sex. Homosexual copulation is as common as heterosexual couplings. Sex is performed in the missionary position as often as any other position, and the couples kiss with their lips and tongue. Sex is not restricted to estrus, but is practiced all through the female menstrual cycle, although the female will initiate sex more frequently when she is in estrus than at other times. Female bonobos have been documented to engage in sex with males in exchange for food.

Here, among these four primate groups, are all the principal elements of human mating behavior. Both the baboons and the chimps form temporary pair bonds based on exchange of resources and protection of the female in return for exclusive sexual access for the male. The gorillas form life-long bonds in a polygynous arrangement. The male gorillas and baboons protect and care for the offspring of the females in their company. Female chimps use sex to turn aside male aggression and to open doors into new social groups. Both bonobos and chimps use their sexuality for a variety of social purposes other than reproduction. Both males and females use sex to establish political alliances and determine rank in their groups. Bonobos, like humans, engage in sex purely for pleasure, or as a form of play. Other, darker attributes are also revealed in these primates, such as the jealousy and spouse abuse seen in the baboons.

All the elements are present and the groundwork is laid. The basic design features are complete for the appearance of early human marriage among primitive hunter-gathers. Here are romance, cooperation, pairing, protection, lust, faithfulness, devotion, compromise, and sex play. Here also are jealousy, oppression, spouse abuse, seduction, intrigue, prostitution, and abandonment.

Pre-Historic Human Marriage

Marriage has been present in human cultures since pre-history. Even the oldest, most primitive human cultures have well-established marriage customs with rules regarding sexual obligations. However, it is important to note that sexual privileges associated with marriage were, and still are, a social bonding device among primitive humans. They are completely unrelated to reproduction. Primitive humans did not engage in sex in order to have children. They did not understand this connection. At the dawn of human history, reproduction was an unrecognized by-product of sexual activities that were undertaken for pleasure and social bonding.

Humans did not acquire knowledge of the relationship between sex and conception until they domesticated animals. Prior to that time, sex was purely a social function. It helped determine who was friendly to whom, who shared food and resources, who stood where in the pecking order of the group, and who would stand where during a group conflict.

Hunter-Gatherer Societies

The Mardu Aborigines in the Western Desert of Australia have a solid understanding of how babies occur. A woman becomes pregnant when a spirit child enters her body through her mouth, nose, or vagina. Spirit children are present all around the Mardu, in the plants and animals and in the sacred places. The Mardu know when a woman receives a spirit child, because she vomits some food that she has eaten. If she eats some kangaroo and vomits, then a spirit child has come from the kangaroo and entered her body. The spirit will grow into a baby, exit her body, and become a person. It will live out a life as a human, and will then return to the spirit world when the human dies.

Like most primitive hunter-gatherers, the Mardu do not recognize any cause and effect relationship between sex and pregnancy. They have no concept of paternity, and no awareness of any part played by the husband in the pregnancy. In fact, they do not even recognize the role played by the mother. They believe that the spirit child feeds itself until birth, and is sometimes accidentally born to the wrong mother.

Mardu Aborigine marriages are arranged between young adult males and prepubescent girls. Mardu children are well aware of sex, and often play sexual games that may even include coitus. A married girl may continue to play these games with other children, but will not begin sexual activity with her husband until she begins to have menses. Sexual relations between a husband and wife are a social obligation among the Mardu, but they are not exclusive, and they have no relationship to pregnancy or childrearing. The Mardu marriages are "open" marriages, in the sense that both partners are free to engage in sex with any other persons they choose. Partners and the community only object if infidelity leads to elopement. Marriages in the Mardu community are arranged years in advance, and are the basis of the social ties within the community. An elopement threatens those social ties. The Mardu have a very liberal view of infidelity, but they view falling in love as a threat to marriages and domestic stability.

Among the Yanomamo, a group of hunter-gatherers in South America, women also become pregnant by enigmatic devices, but men play an important role in the pregnancy.

This culture teaches that the unborn baby is nourished by semen. The healthiest babies are those who are born to mothers who have the most sexual partners during pregnancy. Many men in the community play a role in a woman's pregnancy by providing food to the mother, and feeding her baby through copulation. The actual role of semen in the conception is not understood in the Yanomano culture. All the men who have sex with a woman during her pregnancy are equally responsible for the well being of the baby. The Yanomamo have marriage, and the marriage partners have sexual obligations to each other, but the role of sex in reproduction is not recognized.

The !Kung San, AKA the Kalahari bushmen, are an ancient human population of hunter-gatherers that still live in groups of up to a hundred in the Kalahari Desert in Central Africa. They live a nomadic lifestyle, with each group confined to a territory. They have well-established marriage customs that include both arranged marriages and pair-bonding. The group holds a ceremony to witness a marriage. The first marriage is usually arranged, and is usually short-lived. Subsequent marriages are pair bonds. They last a few years each. Marriages are dissolved privately and informally.

As in other hunter-gather cultures, marriage among the !Kung San is not sexually exclusive. Men and women have sexual obligations to their marriage partners, but both men and women are also free to have sex with whomever they choose. Infidelity is generally done discreetly. Even where promiscuity is the norm, too much blatant infidelity can precipitate conflict with a spouse. In such cultures, jealousy is frowned upon, and the group may actually chastise a male who makes too much fuss over his wife's infidelity. Even so, fighting over women is the most common cause of homicide among the !Kung San.

!Kung San believe that the wife's obligation is to provide sex to the husband and to care for the children. The husband will help in the care of his wife's children to the extent that he wishes, but it is not his obligation. The husband's obligation is to provide meat and other resources for the woman and her children. The wife also provides food in the form of plant products that she gathers. The !Kung San will frankly state that if a wife wants to be rid of her husband she only needs to refuse him sex and he will leave. If a husband wants to be free of his wife he need only stop providing for her and she will abandon him.

Any children from a marriage remain with the mother until weaning, and then are generally raised by the entire group. Like most hunter-gatherer cultures, !Kung San children nurse from their mothers' breast for two to three years, and then are raised by the village. A typical !Kung San adult will have four or five marriages over the course of a lifetime, with one or two children per marriage. Only two of these children, on average, will survive to reproductive age.

Hunter-gatherer cultures are promiscuous, and there is no concept of paternity, as in the Mardu, or a very inaccurate concept, as in the Yanomamo. In these cultures, as in the great apes, incest taboos exist, but are limited by the lack of basic understanding of fatherhood. The taboos restrict women from engaging in sex with their brothers and sons, but not with their fathers, because they do not know the identity of their fathers. Likewise, men do not engage in sex with their sisters or their mothers, but they may engage in sex with their biological daughters, simply because they cannot know which young women in the community are their daughters.

The danger of accidental liaisons between father and daughter persists today among promiscuous humans, and was a sub-plot of the popular movie *Rumor Has It,* starring Jennifer Aniston and Kevin Costner. Released in 2005, the film tells of a brief affair between Sarah and an older man named Beau, which creates havoc when Sarah discovers that her mother had an affair with beau at about the time that she was conceived. She is horrified that she may have accidently had sex with her biological father. Of course, the matter is resolved before the end of the film, but the presence of this theme in a popular film shows a public awareness of this particular social hazard in promiscuous populations.

Hoe-Based Agriculture Societies

About ten thousand years ago, humans began practicing crude agriculture based on the use of a hoe to dig the soil. As humans transitioned from hunter-gatherers to hoe-based agricultural societies, they settled into villages. Women had homes and tended small gardens. They were bound to the land. A woman and her children would till and plant a small plot of land using only hand tools such as hoes and digging sticks.

The women provided most of the vegetable calories in the diet, while men hunted and provided meat for the women and their children. The meat constituted less than half of the calories, but provided most of the dietary protein that is so essential to the health of children. Men also provided other resources and services to earn their keep. Men could physically protect women and their children from wild animals, or from other men. They could handle heavy objects and build shelters.

The women competed with each other for the services of men by advertising their fecundity, through their physical appearance and the number of their existing children. A large number of living children served as an advertisement that a woman would be a good reproductive partner. A woman with many children had many helping hands to work the garden. A woman's value was based on her fecundity, her ability to produce children. Note the contrast to our current cultural norms. Current dogma places high value on the virgin, or at least on the nulliparous woman. Under primitive conditions, when a man considered a woman as a mate, pre-existing children were considered a plus. The woman had proven her ability to produce children, and she had extra hands to help her in the garden and forest.

This marked the emergence of the matrilineal matrilocal pattern that persists today in some areas of Africa. Marriages were informal arrangements in which a man took up residence with a woman for a while, providing for her and her children, while having relatively exclusive sexual access to her. A man would generally have several women with whom he would intermittently reside. Each pair bond continued until he got tired of the domestic life, or until she got tired of him and ran him off. He would then go off to stay by himself, or with another woman for a while. Each woman might have several men who would reside with her intermittently. After one left, another would show up and stay for a while.

None of these men would know which of the women's children were actually his offspring. Each of them would treat all the children as their own. The children would refer to any one of the men in their lives as their father. A woman kept a man close to her by giving him companionship and affection, and he earned his keep by giving her companionship, resources, and protection. Very likely, she would become pregnant by him in the process, and both their genes would be propagated.

Note that up to this point in human history, the females had complete freedom to have sex with whomever they chose. Also note that all wealth, including children, land, and housing, were in the possession of the women. Men were only transients in their lives. This was the reproductive lifestyle to which humans were adapted, whether by evolution or design. Until five thousand years ago, this is how humans naturally paired and reproduced. Let me reiterate this point because it is so important. Up until about five thousand years ago, women were free to have sex with whomever they chose, and women were in complete control of their homes and families. Men were transients in their lives. This is how people are genetically programmed to behave. This is what feels most comfortable to women.

Cows, Plows, and the Demise of Women's Rights

According to Helen Fisher in *The Anatomy of Love*, about five thousand years ago, humans developed plows and large-scale agriculture, and it was a disaster for women. Plowing was done with oxen and horses, and it required the strength of men. Once land was tilled, the land itself became valuable. A piece of valuable land had to be defended from marauders, and defense of the land required men. Large-scale agriculture and animal husbandry concentrated the food production industry into a small portion of the population. It freed people from subsistence hunting and gardening, and allowed the emergence of skilled craftsmen. The products of skilled workers were traded over long distances, and commerce was born. As landowners, craftsmen, and merchants accumulated wealth, they began to obsess about inheritance. Land and wealth had to be defended by men, had to belong to men, and had to be transferred from father to son. Women simply could not compete physically with men either in the tasks of tilling the land with plows, or in military defense of land and wealth.

The role of women changed drastically. Their value was no longer determined by their ability to produce a large number of children, but by their ability to produce children of known paternity. The determinant of a woman's value changed from fecundity to fidelity. A woman was no longer required to be prolific, but rather to be chaste. Women lost the freedom to choose their mates, or to change sexual partners. They lost the freedom to engage in extramarital sex or in premarital sex. They were mandated into abstinence until married. All of their mating choices were made by men. They were forced into strict fidelity to the men who provided their livelihoods. And they were severely punished for any deviation from the rules laid down by men. Women became pieces of the estate. They were the property of their male kin. A woman was subservient not only to her husband/owner, but to her father, brother, and son. Fathers or brothers chose husbands for women. Marriages were contracts between families. The marriage vows were a property deed, not much different than a bill of sale for a slave.

Think of my junior colleague Caroline in this context, and of how drastically culture has changed. The Western world

Various Perspectives on Modern Marriage

The highest happiness on Earth is marriage

William Lyon Phelps

What a happy and holy fashion it is that those who love one another should rest on the same pillow.

Nathanial Hawthorne

I've been married eleven years and I've had three children. I guess that means I breed well in captivity.

Roseanne Barr

Any intelligent woman who reads the marriage contract, and then goes into it, deserves all the consequences.

Isadora Duncan

Marriage Ceremony: An incredible physical sham of watching God and the law being dragged into the affairs of your family.

O.C. Ogilvie

has now abandoned the patriarchal culture that arose after the development of plow based agriculture. Western women now have economic equality. Those who choose to do so can be independent of men. Caroline has pursued an education and a high-paying career. She does not need a man to provide her livelihood, and so she has earned her personal and sexual freedom. She does not need to submit to the rules laid down by men. But Caroline is a new phenomenon, the product of a mere fifty years of divergence from the patriarchal cultures that ruled the world for five thousand years, and still rule half the world.

Women were not the only ones to suffer from the patriarchal cultures. The social systems that arose with the development of the plow also disenfranchised young and poor men. As long as women were free to choose their lovers, a handsome, strong young man would always have some opportunity to mate, no matter how poor he was. But once wealthy, powerful men could own, imprison, and monopolize women, the opportunities for poor men evaporated. They were left with a dwindling supply of less desirable women, or they could join the military and hope for opportunities to kidnap and rape women in occupied territories. All the quality women were wives, mistresses, concubines, or house servants of the wealthy.

The oldest known written laws describing marriage are in the Hammurabi Code, from Babylon, 3,750 years ago. These describe marriage as a commercial transaction for the sale and ownership of women. Husbands bought and sold wives. These women were their property. Men could imprison their wives or put them in chains. A husband could choose a new wife, and downgrade the status of his current wife to that of a household slave.

This is the origin of the marriage traditions that have treated women as property for thousands of years. Although the past century has seen major changes in the Western world, and women are no longer in chastity belts, there are residual traditions that still treat women as property. The old beliefs and values persist as subtle intrusions in our culture. Tradition still dictates that a suitor requests the permission of the bride's father before asking the bride for marriage. The father escorts the bride to the altar, reminiscent of a time when she would not have gone willingly. The father (the current owner) gives away his daughter (his property) to the groom (the new owner). The bride is expected to be a virgin, dressed in white, while the groom is not. The bride is carried across the threshold, reminiscent of a time when she would not have gone into the man's home willingly.

A wife is expected to adhere to absolute fidelity, while the husband is not. In many places today, there are still severe penalties for adultery by the wife, while adultery by the husband is begrudgingly accepted. Adultery by the wife is universally considered grounds for divorce, while adultery by the husband is not. Even in Western cultures today, a wife is still financially penalized for adultery. In most of the United States, the laws regarding spousal support are punitive towards a married woman who exercises sexual freedom. In divorce proceedings a woman who was supported by her husband during the marriage is entitled to continued support after the divorce, in the form of alimony. However, the woman who committed adultery during the marriage loses her alimony.

Gradually, authorities began exercising their own interests in the marriage process. Religious entities became involved about 1000 years ago in Europe, and somewhat earlier in the Middle East and the Far East. About 2000 years ago, the Jewish faith decreed that man and woman were only partial souls, and that they merged through marriage to form a complete soul. About 1300 years ago, Mohammed laid down Allah's rules regarding how many wives a man could have, how he should treat them, and how they should treat him. About 900 years ago, the Catholic Church mandated fidelity as a religious obligation and introduced the concept of "till death do we part."

Marriage had been an institution for many thousands of years before religious authorities intruded into the matter. The idea of "two souls with one thought, two hearts that beat as one" was a relative latecomer to the institution of marriage. Love became a spiritual union, persisting throughout life and after death, only after it was decreed to be so by the Jewish and Christian religious authorities. This is a very important point. Jewish and Christian religious authorities decided just in the past 2000 years that humans should be monogamous.

It is really more complicated than that, though. Civil authorities also took an interest as humans accumulated personal wealth and marriage became a legal device for the transfer of property through inheritance. Transfers of property or money are opportunities for taxation. Civil authorities were interested in the taxes on the inheritance. Also, where land and political power were inherited, marriage became a political tool to create alliances, and those same political authorities insisted that people stayed with the marriage partners assigned to them in order to maintain the power structure. About 1000 years ago in Europe, landlords began to exercise control over peasant marriages as a land-management tool. It has only been in the past 400 years that local governments began to actually register and license marriages in Europe. The main emphasis of these efforts was to regulate inheritance and collect taxes. Today, governmental interest in marriage focuses primarily on protection of the rights of any children born in the marriage, but this is a very modern innovation. Until a century ago, governments did not show any interest in the welfare of children. They were only interested in the political and financial consequences of marriage.

Bastards don't inherit!

Ken Follet, *Fall of Giants*

Enforcement of Fidelity

As wealth and centralized political power accumulated, the motivation to enforce marriage vows increased. The emphasis of this enforcement effort was the absolute control of paternity. The husband must always be the father of any children of the marriage.

Paternity is not easy to control. The maternity of a child is never in question. Everyone in the community knows whose birth canal delivered a baby. Paternity is not so certain. Restrictions had to be placed on women in order to ensure that any child born to a woman was indeed fathered by her husband. This is why a double standard in sexual freedoms arose from the cultural transition that occurred 5000 years ago. When inheritances were involved, the paternity of the heirs needed to be controlled at all costs, but the costs were mostly levied upon the females.

Marriage did not grant a man's property to a woman, but it did grant that property to the children she bore while she was married to him. The wealth that a man and his ancestors had accumulated must not go to another man's offspring. It became essential that husbands prevent any opportunity for their wives to become pregnant by other men. The husbands must not be cuckolded. From the male point of view, a married woman who bore a male child of a man other than her husband was committing an act of great thievery. She was stealing all the accumulated wealth of her husband and all his ancestors, and, from his point of view, she deserved severe punishment.

This belief, that men should be able to control who impregnates the women in their community, is profoundly flawed. It stands in stark defiance of natural order. It is an attempt to override sexual selection. Under natural conditions, females are supposed to decide which males reproduce, and males are supposed to decide which females reproduce. The modern rules of marriage, which apply fidelity only to females, attempt to usurp the natural privileges of the females. It is a violation of some very basic rules of biology.

The determination of men to pursue this course of action has caused some very peculiar, and sometimes gruesome, consequences in the historical record. Some cultures have encouraged infanticide of first-born children. Both men and women have been imprisoned or mutilated. Cruel and horrible punishments have been meted out, all in the name of preserving the legitimacy of heirs. Countless women have been executed for the crime of adultery, and the practice still continues today in some cultures, most recently under the fundamentalist Muslim regime in Iran. European Christendom put women in locked iron chastity belts for years at a time. Some extant Islamic cultures still keep women imprisoned, and force them to wear burqas, which are basically monocolored sacks with a mesh over the eyes so the women can look out. In additional to being uncomfortable, these outer garments are completely depersonalizing. Female genital mutilation persists in much of Africa and the Middle East. This renders the female incapable of enjoying sex, and often makes sex extremely painful. In some cultures, the wife's labia majora are sewn together. The stitches are released only long enough for the husband to have sex with her, and then the opening is re-sewn.

The use of barbaric methods to control sexuality in females has not been limited to Muslims. Clitorectomy, the surgical removal of the clitoris, was an accepted treatment for a wide range of female childhood maladies, including excessive sexuality in young girls in Victorian England and the United States until well into the twentieth century. The last well-respected medical textbook to recommend clitorectomy as a treatment of female childhood masturbation was published in 1936. It was only a mere eighty years ago that genital mutilation of females was still prescribed in England and the United States.

Women were not the only victims of the drive to suppress female sexuality. Soldiers were needed to guard wives, but soldiers could not be trusted around women, and visa versa. Castration of security guards in wealthy private households was a common practice in some cultures until only a few decades ago. Sometimes this involved only removal of the testicles, and sometimes the entire genitalia were amputated.

Just as there were harsh penalties for female adultery, there were equally severe consequences for the male caught in a compromising situation with the wife of a wealthy, powerful man. If the intruding male did manage to escape death, he would, at best, end up as a household security guard with a high-pitched voice.

Termination of Marriage

Wherever there has been marriage, there has also been divorce. In most primitive cultures, either party to a marriage could end it, and the process was often informal. Until the last century, most post-Neolithic cultures only allowed the men to initiate divorce. Men have universally been allowed to divorce women who engaged in adultery. However, adultery has rarely been accepted as a cause for women to divorce their husbands. Conversely, non-support has been widely accepted as a cause for women to divorce their husbands, but has never been a cause for husbands to divorce their wives. Generally, where marriage has been an informal arrangement, divorce has been casual. Late in the game, after religious and civil authorities became involved in marriage, these authorities also exercised some control over divorce.

In those cultures where men owned everything, a woman left the marriage with nothing. She might have been returned to her parents, or she might have simply been put out. Some cultures allowed her to be downgraded to a household slave. In some cultures a woman's jewelry and her dowry were her own property. In others, she might retain her inheritance from her parents. In matrilineal matrilocal societies, the children stayed with their mother. In patrilineal cultures, children were the property of the father. They did not remain with the mother unless they were thought to be the offspring of an adulterous union. This remained the case well into the nineteenth century.

The Current State of Marriage

As we enter the twenty-first century, almost everything has changed. The past century has witnessed tremendous upheaval in the traditions of marriage and in reproductive behavior in general in the Western world. Young people who read this paragraph today cannot possibly fathom the changes that have occurred since 1920, when American women were finally allowed to exercise their right to vote. Until a mere ninety years ago, women, even in the United States, were not full citizens. By contrast, women in the Western world today choose their own sexual partners, make their own reproductive decisions, and can exercise complete control over when and whether they become pregnant and by whom. Women can no longer be forced into marriage in Europe or anywhere in the Western hemisphere. They choose their own spouses and lovers. They need the consent of their parents only if they are juveniles. The practice of child betrothal has been illegalized in the Western world and in much of Asia.

Nonetheless, arranged-marriage customs persist in large areas of the world. Some nations and religions still allow the reproductive choices of both males and females to be made by relatives, without any regard for the feelings of the soon-to-be sexual partners. In the Hindu culture today, there are eight types of marriage, and seven of them are arranged by relatives. The arrangements usually include exchanges of money or property. That may seem to some people like selling children into slavery, but it is a sustained cultural tradition.

Huge, insurmountable cultural differences persist all around us, and we usually do not see them. One recent morning I was exiting the hospital cafeteria as a young woman approached the same door from the other side, and opened it simultaneously with me. As often happens, an instant of confusion ensued regarding who was opening the door for whom. She conceded and passed through first, thus allowing me to be the one who had opened the door for her. I suppose a tiny remnant of chivalry, and perhaps inequality, still persists.

For some reason, in that instant, I was impressed by how familiar and unremarkable this little drama was in the Western culture, and at the same time, how impossible it would be in some cultures. This young woman is a co-worker, and is on essentially equal social standing with me. She has the same right as I do to pass through the door first, and the same right to open the door for me. The decision is hers as much as it is mine. She is a free person, a full citizen. She is dressed in slacks and a simple blouse, presumably because that is the outfit she chose. That decision is also hers. She is unmarried. She is walking to the cafeteria alone. She is employed in the profession of her choice. She went to college to learn the job. She works for her living and supports herself.

These are all things that are disallowed in the fundamentalist Muslim cultures, and in many other reactionary religious cultures around the world, where women are still forbidden from leaving their homes without a male family member, or from driving, or from working outside the home. The Muslim marriage contract stipulates the woman's obligation to bear children for her husband, and a woman who uses birth control without the husband's consent is committing a breach of her contract. Under Sharia Law, wives have no property rights and few enforceable legal rights. A woman who is raped is presumed guilty of adultery and may be imprisoned. Women may not testify in court, even on their own behalf. If they are allowed to speak, their testimony is severely restricted and has diminished value. A wife is helpless. In 2009, a United Nations resolution supporting human rights was defeated because Muslim nations interpreted it as prohibiting a man from beating a wife who refuses him sex.

The conflict between the Judeo-Christian and Islamic religions is almost entirely centered on the human rights of women. When the United States entered the Afghanistan theater, the rallying point focused on the Taliban mistreatment of women. Images flashed across the TV screens, to be burned into our memories, of Taliban thugs beating women with nightsticks while the women cowered in their burkas. War widows begged in the streets for money to feed their starving children because they were not allowed to work or remarry. According to their fundamentalist beliefs, the Taliban were carrying out their responsibility of keeping the women in their community faithful to the will of Allah.

When the Ayatollah Khomeini called the United States "The Great Satan," he was referring to the lax morality of Western culture. In the Muslim culture, Satan is a seducer, one who corrupts others by setting a bad example. When the fundamentalist Muslims look upon the Western society, they have the same response that the British upper class had when they witnessed bare-breasted African native women. They see us as heathen barbarians. From the fundamentalist Muslim point of view, Western women walk around in public half naked, exposing their bodies to every passing male, without any chaperones to secure their fidelity. They talk to any male they choose, spend time alone with whomever they choose, and engage in sex with whomever they choose. They work if they want, travel where they want, provide for themselves, and do as they please. The Sunni Muslim wonders how faithful Muslim women can be expected to adhere to the moral standards given by Allah to his true prophet, Mohammed, when they witness such immoral behavior among Western women. The answer, of course, is that they cannot. When given the opportunity, most Muslim women quickly abandon the restrictions of the fundamentalist Islam culture.

The corollary is that the Western world offends fundamentalist Muslims not because of the actions of Western nations, but rather because of the very existence of the Western culture. It is intolerable. The fundamentalist Muslims cannot live in peace with Westerners. Their religious beliefs, particularly those regarding women's rights, make peaceful co-existence impossible. The war between fundamentalist Muslims and the West, which is currently being fought all over the world, is the direct result of the difficulties that human males incur in their efforts to control the reproductive choices of human females. Human sexuality has wide-ranging social, political, and military repercussions.

The Western world has seen tremendous upheaval in the past century. Wives are no longer the property of husbands, but are on equal standing, legally and economically. Women are rapidly regaining the freedom and power they had before the invention of the plow and the domestication of cattle. In the process, women are also regaining control of human reproduction. The history of marriage over the past 5000 years has been a tale of struggle between men and women as to who controls the paternity of offspring. Western cultures are returning to the ancient ways in which the females choose which males reproduce, just as the peahens choose which peacocks will reproduce. Perhaps this 5000-year-long night-mare for women is finally ending.

When human females have sexual freedom, they control which males fertilize their ova, and that is the subject of the next chapter.

10

The Complex Female Orgasm

When modern woman discovered orgasm, it was, combined with birth control, perhaps the biggest single nail in the coffin of male dominance.

EVA FIGS

The last chapter reviewed men's struggle to gain control over women's reproductive choices. This is not an easy task. Women are designed in a way that gives them a great deal of control over who fertilizes their ova, even though they are not aware of the process. This chapter will look at women's tools in the struggle.

The human female is a tough opponent. She has devices at her disposal that even she does not understand. Her time of fertility is hidden and brief, but she is sexually active all through her monthly hormone cycle. She is genetically programmed to use her sexuality to obtain resources from many males while discreetly choosing the male who will fertilize her eggs. For the most part, this occurs without any aware-ness on her part.

All human mating behavior, beginning with the first inquisitive eye contact, is part of a social dance that leads, if successful, to the act of sex. It is all part of a complicated sort-ing process during which males choose females, and females choose males. But the competition and selection do not stop when sex occurs.

The physiology of sex is complex, and a lot of activity is going on under the surface, literally and figuratively. While lovers are engaged in the mechanics of bumping and grind-ing, the internal genitalia are busy, too. The male is focused on delivering his gametes, but he is also unwittingly perform-ing other functions. The female is not just a passive receptacle for sperm. Her body can utilize the semen of different males selectively, based, in part, on her motives for having sex with them.

It can be difficult to decide just where to begin a discus-sion of copulation. A long chain of events leads up to sex. Lovers have to first overcome social hurdles and ego bound-aries. This chapter begins at the point where the lovers are disrobed, with their limbs intertwined, each trying to maneu-ver the other into a favorable position.

The male has a ready supply of sperm in his vas defer-ens, the tubes leading from the testicles. He has also gen-erated a supply of seminal fluid in the prostate. His penis is engorged with blood, filling the various compartments until the longitudinal and circumferential strands of con-nective tissue are stretched tight, making the organ rigid. His heart rate and breathing rate are increased. All the mus-cles in his body are tense, and his senses are heightened. The primitive senses of touch, smell, and taste are ampli-fied. His brain is focused on the feelings in his skin, espe-cially on the mouth and genitalia, but also on his hands, and all over his body.

In the female, things are more complicated. Her physi-ology varies according to her hormonal state, which is dependent on her place in the menstrual cycle. The female in estrus, near time of ovulation, is more likely to be motivated by pleasure. Her mindset at this point in her cycle is much like that of the male, who is driven by simple lust. The female who is not in estrus may also feel lust, or she may be having sex for ulterior motives completely unrelated to her pleasure. Unlike a male, the female can engage in sex when not aroused. Assuming she is aroused, her genitalia are also swollen and engorged, although it is not as obvious as in the male. Both sexes have genital organs of the same basic design. The female has the same compartments engorged with blood as the male. He has the penis and its related structures, while she has the clitoris and its related structures, and both work the same way. Hers are smaller than his, but they are equally entertaining.

Her vagina is excreting a lubricating fluid from pores in the walls, wetting the entire internal surface. Her Bartholin's glands, small glands opening on the inside walls of the labia minora, at the opening of the vagina, are secreting a substance that looks and feels like a high-quality hand lotion. The labia majora and labia minora are swollen and separated. This opens the door of the vagina, allowing easy entrance by the penis.

If all goes well, as the lovers maneuver each other into position, he has no difficulty finding her vagina, and she has no difficulty admitting him. If he is uncircumcised, his foreskin will contact her labia, and his glans will easily slide through his foreskin and into the vaginal opening. If he is circumcised, he may meet some resistance when pushing the swollen glans past the labia, unless he has allowed enough time for the Bartholin's glans to do their job thoroughly.

If they are in the missionary position, she flexes her hips and spreads her knees wide apart. He spreads his knees apart and flexes his hips, so that he supports his weight on his arms and knees, and his thighs push hers up and apart. She may put her legs behind him, clasping him and pulling him to her. He alternately flexes and relaxes his lower back, advancing and retracting his penis from her vagina. This stimulates the skin on his penis, the skin and mucosa of her labia, and the mucosa in the vagina, causing pleasurable sensations.

As their excitement increases, he increases the speed and frequency of his thrusting into her vagina. He may have sudden involuntary thrusts, striking his mons pubis rather firmly against her vulva, and striking her cervix with the end of his penis, causing fairly rough movement of her internal pelvic organs. He may press himself firmly against her vulva, rocking his mons pubis against her external genitalia.

As she becomes more excited, she spreads her thighs wider, and tilts her pelvis up. She flexes her low back rhythmically, and rubs her genitals, especially her clitoris, against his mons pubis and the base of his penis. As she nears climax, her clitoris becomes hard and swollen. As the small, firm clitoris touches against the dorsal surface of the base of his penis, it stimulates him to climax.

If he is behind her, she may be standing, leaning over something, or down on her hands and knees, or even lying prone. She arches her low back and pushes her buttocks back against him. If she is standing, she rises up on her toes and tilts her pelvis backward, exposing her external genitalia rearward and giving him access to her vaginal opening. The male mons and penis do not contact the clitoris in this position, and many women will not climax in this position unless they stimulate the clitoris with their fingers.

However, many women favor this position for lovemaking. It provides for deeper penetration, which is pleasurable if the male's penis is not too long. Also, many women have an exceptionally sensitive area in the front wall of the vagina, the G-spot, which will cause them to orgasm when it is stimulated. Rear entry rubs directly on this area.

The Truth about Penis Size

This is a good time to mention two other points of interest. Penis size does matter, but not in the way that most people think. Women vary remarkably in the size of the vagina, and women with greater body fat have less accessible vaginas. Some women have large, deep vaginas. Those women with deep vaginas, or with heavy body habitus, will generally prefer men with longer penises. However, thin women, or women with small vaginas, or women with sensitive pelvic interiors due to disease or scarring, will definitely prefer men with smaller penises. There really is such a thing as too big, and it can be very uncomfortable for a woman. In size of genitalia, as with everything else, the man and woman should be well matched.

Some European historians believe that the French revolution was caused in part by a mismatch in size. King Louis XVI and Marie Antoinette were unable to produce an heir for the first eight years of their marriage because they were unable to engage in sex. Louis was endowed with a "bracquemart assez considerable," while Marie had "l'etroitesse du chemin." That is to say, he had a large penis, and she had a small vagina, and they were unable to make love comfortably. The long delay in production of an heir prevented the formation of a strong military alliance between the Bourbons and the Hapsburgs, and the monarchy of France collapsed under the revolution.

The Para-urethral Gland

The second point of interest is the G-spot. This is actually the location of the para-urethral gland around the urethra on the front wall of the vagina. The gland secretes fluid to moisten and lubricate the interior of the tube that leads from the bladder to the outside world. It is the equivalent of the prostate gland in the male, but is much smaller. Like the prostate gland, it can be a source of pleasurable sensations when massaged. The size of the para-urethral gland is highly variable from one woman to the next. Some women have none at all while others may be well endowed. This is why some women respond to stimulation of the G-spot and others do not. It is also why some women enjoy rear-entry sex more than others.

The para-urethral gland also secretes fluid, and a woman with a large amount of para-urethral gland tissue can disgorge a large volume of fluid at orgasm, just like the male disgorging fluid from the prostate gland to produce semen. This is the source of the female ejaculate that some women produce. The variability in the size of the para-urethral gland is the reason that some women ejaculate and others do not.

Female ejaculation remains a controversial subject in modern literature, with many researches denying that it occurs. However, it must be remembered that, until the studies by Masters and Johnson in the 1960s, many scientists and physicians thought that the female orgasm was a myth. The history of both female orgasm and female ejaculation goes back into antiquity. Aristotle (384 – 322 B.C.E.) discussed both phenomena, as did the Greek physician Galen of Pergamon (129 – 199 C.E.). In Muslin antiquity, according to the Tabitha, when Muhammad was asked what determines whether a child will look like the father or the mother, he responded, "If a man has sexual intercourse with his wife and gets discharge first, the child will resemble the father, and if a woman gets discharge first, the child will resemble her." The Tabitha was recorded by Muhammed ibn Ismail al-Bukhari (810 – 870 C.E.), about 200 years after the death of Muhammad, so we have no way of knowing whether this record is historically accurate. However, it is certain that the individual who recorded it knew that human females sometimes have a liquid discharge at the climax of sexual intercourse.

The existence of the female orgasm is likewise well known to primitive peoples. The !Kung San woman chastises a man who climaxes and then leaves her unsatisfied. If he does not complete his task, she will go and find someone who will.

The unsatisfactory male may thus lose his opportunity to reproduce.

During the Climax

Returning to the act of copulation, other interesting things are happening. As the couple approaches orgasm, their genitalia become more engorged. His penis grows larger and firmer, and the glans swells. Also, his scrotum contracts and pulls his testicles close against his body. Her clitoris also swells, but just before orgasm, it retracts under the clitoral hood.

If the female has semen left in her vaginal vault from sex with a prior male, her current lover removes it before he ejaculates. The shape of the glans on his penis, with its rounded point and flared rim, acts like a bilge pump. As he thrusts and withdraws, his penis is removing any liquid from the vaginal vault. The human male with an adequately sized penis will remove his adversary's semen from a female's vagina. The previous male, who left the woman unsatisfied, thus loses his chance to reproduce. This is one of the mechanisms that favors the male with a larger diameter penis, and is probably one of the reasons that human males have the largest-diameter penis of all primates.

If the female is near ovulation, she has a cyst on her ovary. In human females, the ovum grows in a small fluid-filled chamber on the surface of the ovary. It requires two months to mature. Most women alternate right and left ovaries from month to month, but some women form ova in both ovaries every month, and these are the women who can have fraternal twins. As the ovum ripens, the fluid-filled chamber enlarges to about one-half inch in diameter, to become a specialized, thin-walled cyst, called the ovulatory cyst.

When the ovum is mature, the cyst waits patiently on the ovary for several days. Eventually, it ruptures spontaneously, and that is called ovulation. When this cyst ruptures, the ovum is spilled out onto the fimbria, which is a patch of soft carpet-like tissue on the end of the fallopian tube. Sometimes ovulation hurts, and some women can tell every month exactly when they have ovulated.

The ovum and the fluid in the cyst contain chemicals that attract sperm. When ovulation occurs, these chemicals diffuse outward, and form a gradient or a trail for the sperm to follow to the ovum.

The rough jumbling of a woman's internal pelvic organs during copulation may rupture an ovulatory cyst, causing ovulation to occur during sex. The male who is engaged in sex with her at the time is then more likely to be the one to fertilize her ovum and impregnate her. He who has a long enough penis to rupture her ovulatory cyst becomes the winner. This mechanism selects for the males most able to induce females to ovulate during intercourse and is another reason why the human male has a large penis.

The male climax consists of several stages, but the end result is that the sperm in the vas deferens combine with the seminal fluid in the seminal vesicles and prostate. This mixture is propelled through the urethra by a series of peristaltic waves, and is deposited in the vaginal vault near the cervix. At the same time, many other muscles in the pelvis and genitalia spasm rhythmically, and muscles of the back and limbs contract powerfully. The male experiences an overwhelming sensation of pleasure, and his oxytocin level immediately increases to five times the resting level.

The female climax is similar in many ways to that of the male. Her body responds in the same manner as his, with rhythmic spasms of the muscles in the pelvis and powerful contractions of the limb and back muscles. Her genital organs are also busy during orgasm. The vaginal opening contracts, while the vault relaxes. The cervix and uterus undergo peristaltic waves, pumping semen to the fallopian tubes. And, of course, she experiences extreme pleasure, with a five-fold increase in oxytocin.

It should be kept in mind that primitive people had no knowledge of these processes, and, for the most part, neither do modern humans. When people have sex, they are mostly in it for the oxytocin boost. If you ask individuals *why* they have sex, the most common answer is, "Because it feels good."

If everything goes right, the male's thrusting jostles the uterus and ovaries, and ruptures the ovulatory cyst, releasing the ovum onto the fimbria of the fallopian tube. The two lovers both have orgasms. The male ejaculates, depositing sperm and seminal fluid in the vagina, near the cervix. The cervix and uterus draw up the semen and transport the sperm up the fallopian tubes. Over the next ten minutes or so, the sperm swim the rest of the way to the fimbria, following the trail of chemical attractants secreted by the ovum. One sperm will penetrate and fertilize the ovum. The membrane of the ovum immediately seals itself, preventing any further sperm entry. The fallopian tube then transports the fertilized ovum to the uterus over the next several days. The developing embryo implants in the wall of the uterus, and starts the process of developing into a baby.

If the woman has an orgasm, her uterine contractions transport the sperm to the fallopian tubes by peristalsis. It is an active process on her part, and a passive process on the part of the sperm. Then the sperm have to swim the last few centimeters of the journey, following a trail of chemicals. This last part of the journey is a race, and selects for the swift and strong, leaving any defective sperm far behind and out of luck. If the woman has not had an orgasm, then the sperm are on their own to swim the entire distance from the cervix up the uterus, into the fallopian tubes, and up to the fimbria.

Of course, the great majority of copulations do not proceed in this fashion because most sex does not occur when the woman is ovulating. The human female is able to get pregnant for about twenty-four hours out of her twenty-eight-day menstrual cycle, but she can be sexually active for the entire twenty-eight days.

Non-Reproductive Sex

So what is the function of all the sex that is occurring during the non-reproductive portion of a woman's monthly cycle? The great majority of creatures do not have sex for any reason except to create offspring. Unlike most other animals, humans have sex for many reasons other than procreation. They have sex to pleasure themselves, to pleasure each other, to cement relationships, to heal relationships after a rift, and to reward their partners for various behaviors. Both men and women have sex for pure entertainment. Men have sex to dominate women, and women have sex to dominate men. Women trade sex for services, resources, or money. Women have sex to obtain favorable social relationships, or to secure positions. Both men and women have sex in order to meet marital or religious obligations. Both men and women engage in sex to support their own egos, to heal their own hurts, to distract themselves from other worries, or to stave off loneliness.

The Difference between a Mistress, a Prostitute, and a Wife

The mistress lies on her back during sex and thinks, "Oh! Harder! Harder!"

The prostitute lies on her back and thinks, "Faster, faster ..."

The wife lies on her back and thinks, "Beige. I think I'll paint the ceiling beige."

Here is an entirely plausible story of three women having sex for three different reasons, none of which have anything to do with reproduction. The first is intent on pleasure, the second is earning a living, and the third is simply meeting a marital obligation.

In their article, "Why Humans Have Sex," Cindy Meston and David Buss identified 237 different reasons that people gave for having sex. The following table lists ninety-three of them.

Why people have sex

Here are some of the reasons given by college students, mostly single, ranging in age from 17 to 52 years of age, for having sex. Adapted from Meston, Arch Sex Behav (2007) 36:477-507.

I was attracted to the person	It feels good
I wanted to experience the physical pleasure	I wanted to express my love
I wanted to show my affection	I was horny
I realized I was in love	I wanted to achieve an orgasm
I wanted to please my partner	The person's appearance turned me on
I wanted the pure pleasure	I was in the heat of the moment
It is exciting, adventurous	The person really desired me
The person caressed me	I wanted to feel connected to the person
I wanted to become one with the person	It was a romantic setting
I wanted to increase the emotional bond	The person made me feel sexy

I wanted the adventure, excitement

I wanted to keep my partner happy

The person was a good kisser

The opportunity presented itself

My hormones were out of control

I wanted to intensify the relationship

I wanted to feel loved

I wanted to reproduce

To celebrate a special event

I was curious about my sexual abilities

I was curious about sex

I was drunk

The person was intelligent

The person seemed self confident

To keep my partner satisfied

I wanted to experiment

I wanted to improve my sexual skills

The person had beautiful eyes

I wanted to give some one an STD

I wanted to get a favor from someone

I wanted to get a raise

I wanted to punish myself

I wanted to get a job

It was a special occasion

The person offered me drugs for it

Someone offered me money to do it

I wanted to humiliate the person

I wanted to make money

I wanted to break up my relationship

I was angry

I wanted to be used or degraded

Because of a bet

I wanted to get a favor from someone

It would get me gifts

It was a favor to someone

To ruin rival's relationship via sex with his partner

The person had lots of money

I wanted to have more sex than my friends

I thought it would boost my social status

I wanted to stop my partner's nagging

I felt sorry for the person

I had not had sex in a long time

I am a sex addict

So I could focus on other things

The person was mysterious

I wanted to feel older

I wanted to get a promotion

I wanted to relieve menstrual cramps

I wanted to get rid of a headache

To get revenge on partner who cheated

To gain access to that person's friend

I was physically forced to

The person bought me jewelry

My friends pressured me into it

To avoid hurting someone's feelings

The person smelled nice

I thought it would relax me

I wanted to act out a fantasy

An erotic movie had turned me on

I wanted to feel closer to God

I wanted to keep warm	I thought it would help me fall asleep
I wanted to have a child	The person bought me an expensive dinner
I wanted to hurt an enemy	I wanted to reaffirm my sexual orientation
I was married and you are supposed to	I wanted to say "I'm sorry."
I wanted to feel younger	I wanted to make up after a fight
I was feeling lonely	

Most sex in humans is initiated by the male, who is relatively insensitive to the female's desires. Men want sex uniformly throughout the month. They do not have a hormone cycle. They are not aware of, or have only very indirect clues to, when a woman is in estrus. Women can enjoy sex during most of the month, but they feel the strongest physical urge to seek out a sex partner only on those few days of the month when they are in estrus, that is, when they are near ovulation.

As a woman approaches ovulation, and her ovum matures in the cyst on the ovary, the levels of the hormone estradiol rise in her blood stream. This is the female equivalent of testosterone. It stimulates her libido, and puts her in estrus. While it is elevated, she will have increased sex drive, increased tendency to roam, and increased ease and frequency of orgasms. Estradiol causes a woman to seek out sex for her own pleasure. This is the time that the human female is most inclined to search for an attractive opportunistic partner.

Why Women Have Orgasms

The human female orgasm is an enigma. It is not necessary for reproduction. Women can get pregnant without orgasms. They can enjoy sex without orgasms. Men have to have orgasms in order to deliver their ejaculate to the vagina, but women do not have to have them at all. What function or functions does the female orgasm serve, and how does it help humans survive? Some researchers believe that it is just a vestigial function that some women retain because men have orgasms, in the same way that men have nipples because women need breasts. That seems blatantly sexist, a remnant of the Victorian era when the female function in sex was considered strictly that of a passive receptacle. But female organs are not passive, and the orgasm is not a vestigial, shriveled organ like an appendix or the male nipple. It is a highly complex process. Such functions are not retained unless they somehow aid in reproductive success.

There are many theories about the purpose of the female orgasm. They are all flawed because they begin by assuming that there is only one function for female orgasm. In *The Case of the Female Orgasm*, Elizabeth Lloyd reviews the arguments for and against twenty-one theories. She concludes that the orgasm in women is superfluous, and is really not necessary for reproduction. This is true, but it is not the same as saying that the orgasm does not serve a useful purpose. Indeed, human females can get pregnant and reproduce without ever having an orgasm, and many do. However, there are at least two purposes for the female orgasm that are undeniable.

A man is not selective about sex. He has little risk and practices little discretion. A woman, on the other hand, bears the brunt of the work in raising children, and can produce only a few offspring over the course of her life. Just as importantly, a woman's decision is irreversible. Once she becomes pregnant, she is saddled with the lifetime responsibility of raising the child, while the man can just walk away. It is in the best interest of the woman, and of the human species, that she exercises as much control as possible over who fertilizes her ova.

Recall the peacock. Ultimately, the reason the peacock has those big tail feathers is because that is what the peahen wants. The peahen is finicky, and she is the one who does the choosing. This is how it has to be. The human female, who bears the burden of childrearing, must be the one who selects the male gametes. But how is she going to control which male fertilizes her ova when she is having sex with other males for other reasons? The solution to this problem lies partly in the orgasm.

Some women say they never have orgasms. Others say they always have orgasms. Neither is true. What is true is that women are highly variable in their propensity to have orgasms. But even the most disinterested woman, if she is healthy, will orgasm if she is given the proper devoted attention by her Prince Charming (or Princess Charming). And even the most libidinous woman will not orgasm during sex under conditions that are repulsive to her. The one indisputable fact about the female orgasm is that all women are selective about when and with whom they have orgasms.

Combine this information with the estradiol issue, and the purpose of the orgasm becomes clear. A woman is more inclined to search out a lover when she nears ovulation, and she is more likely to choose a sexual partner based on his attractiveness. Her elevated estradiol levels and his attractiveness make her more likely to orgasm with him, and more likely to transport a large number of his sperm to the fallopian tubes, just at the time that she is ovulating. If his penis is large enough and she is near enough to ovulation, and the sex is rough enough, he will rupture her ovulatory cyst during coitus, and she will be pregnant about ten minutes after they climax.

A woman may have sex with her proper mate ten times a month, and with an illicit lover once a month, yet she is more likely to be impregnated by the lover. Of course, it is not a sure thing, but the man she chooses on the basis of pure lust has a definite advantage. Meanwhile, she gets the best of both worlds. She gets all the benefits she has accrued from having sex with her regular partner(s), and she still gets to choose the genetics of her offspring. The other males are none the wiser because they are completely unaware of her cycle. Every male who has copulated with her prior to her liaison with her lover, or who copulates with her during her pregnancy, may help her raise the child.

The Joke is on the Butcher

Many years had passed years since the embarrassing day when a young woman, with a baby in her arms, entered the butcher's shop. She confronted him with the news that the baby was his and asked what he was going to do about it. He offered to provide her with free meat until the boy was sixteen. She agreed.

He had been counting the years off on his calendar, and one day the teenager, who had been collecting the meat each week, came into the shop and said, "I'll be sixteen tomorrow."

"I know," said the butcher with a smile, "I've been counting too. Tell your mother, when you take this parcel of meat home, that it is the last free meat she'll get, and watch the expression on her face."

When the boy arrived home he told his mother. The woman nodded and said, "Son, go back to the butcher and tell him I have also had free bread, free milk, and free produce for the last sixteen years, and watch the expression on his face!"

In the social setting of high promiscuity, such as among the Yanomamo, it is in the best interest of the female to increase her sexual activity during early pregnancy for just this reason. The more sexual partners she has, the more men who may provide her with resources. This may be why her breast size increases so early in pregnancy. She becomes more voluptuous and attractive, and attracts more male attention. The more sexual partners she has, the more fathers her child has. Among some primitive peoples of the world, it is still common practice today for women to acknowledge multiple men as the fathers of a child, because they were all sexual partners to her while she was carrying the pregnancy.

The Female Control of Paternity

Of course, the great majority of modern human females are not so promiscuous, and do not rely on multiple men for their support. Today, the paternity of most children is known. However, the genes that drive human instincts today are the same genes that survived and prospered in Paleolithic times. The anatomy and physiology that is in play in humans today originated when human reproduction was chaotic and highly promiscuous. Humans are still designed the same way, and those same behaviors quickly re-emerge in times of stress, whether it is due to war, natural disaster, or personal crisis. Separation of sexual functions from reproduction does not change the instincts that drive reproduction.

While the subject of promiscuity is still near at hand, it is worthwhile to review the matter of sperm competition. A thorough study of the subject can be found in the book, *Sperm Wars*, by Robin Baker. The essential lesson is that a great deal of male-male competition for the opportunity to fertilize the female's ovum occurs inside the female after two or more males have copulated with her in quick succession.

Paternal discrepancy refers to a situation in which a woman gives birth to a child who is not the offspring of her husband. It is now easily detectable using DNA analysis. In England, a study was undertaken of fraternal twins, that is, twins who are the product of a simultaneous dual ovulation, with each ovum fertilized by one sperm. In one out of every 400 sets of fraternal twins, the two children were fathered by different men. This means that one out of every 200 women who had fraternal twins was inseminated by two different men within three days. Of course, women who bear fraternal twins are no different morally or ethically from women who bear single infants. So the researchers concluded that one out of every two hundred pregnancies in England is of uncertain paternity because the woman's fallopian tubes contained sperm from two or more men when she was impregnated.

Another study, also in England, questioned married women as to whether, at any time in their lives, they had been inseminated by two men within a thirty minute time interval. One out of every two hundred women said they had been. When the time interval was raised to twenty-four hours, thirty percent responded affirmatively. When the time was raised to three days, seventy percent said yes. Sperm usually survive for three days inside a woman. This means that seventy out of every hundred women in the study group had, at some time in their lives, risked a pregnancy of uncertain paternity.

Even in England, a modern industrialized nation dominated by Judeo-Christian cultures, the level of promiscuity is high enough to generate competition between male gametes inside the pelvis of a majority of females at some time in their lives. In that kind of competitive setting, any advantage is significant. The male who stimulates the female to orgasm has a considerable edge over the male who does not, for two reasons. One is that she retains more of his sperm, so his gametes outnumber those of his adversaries. The other is that she is more likely to choose him the next time she goes looking for a lover. After all, it really comes down to whom she chooses.

And that is the other indisputable purpose for the female orgasm. It identifies Prince Charming, the one who does it for her. This is the one who spends the time and has the moves she needs to make sex worth the effort. This is the one who rewards her, who gives her the best return on the social capital that she puts at risk when she exposes herself physically and emotionally to another person. And this is the one she will come back to when she is in estrus and is looking for a lover.

Who's Your Daddy

One Sunday morning, William burst into the living room and said, "Dad! Mom! I have some great news for you! I am getting married to the most beautiful girl in town. She lives a block away and her name is Susan."

After dinner, William's dad took him aside. "Son, I have to talk with you. Your mother and I have been married for thirty years. She's a wonderful wife, but she has never offered much excitement in the bedroom, so I used to fool around with women a lot. Susan is actually your half-sister, and I'm afraid you can't marry her."

William was heartbroken. After eight months, he eventually started dating girls again. A year later, he came home and very proudly announced, "Diane said yes! We're getting married in June."

Again his father insisted on a private conversation and broke the sad news. "Diane is your half-sister too, William. I'm awfully sorry about this."

William was furious! He finally decided to go to his mother with the news.

"Dad has done so much harm. I guess I'm never going to get married," he complained. "Every time I fall in love, Dad tells me the girl is my half-sister."

His mother just shook her head. "Don't pay any attention to what he says, dear. He's not your real father."

The female orgasm has far-ranging social and political implications. When men first tried to seize control of paternity, this is what they were up against. Women are adept at selecting the paternity of their offspring, and they do so in a manner that is completely mysterious to men. In trying to control paternity of women's offspring, men were defying the natural order of things. In their ignorance and determination, men committed, and are still committing, a host of human-rights violations. These reveal the insecurity that men feel in the face of their chief adversaries -- their own wives.

Other Possible Roles for the Female Orgasm

The adaptive theory states that the female orgasm serves the purpose of encouraging women to have sex. This theory has some problems. Women have sex and get pregnant in the absence of orgasms. Ten to twenty percent of women never have orgasms in the setting of heterosexual coitus. Many of the women who do have orgasm with sex do so by digital manipulation of the clitoris (assisted coitus). That is to say, they masturbate while having sex with a man. Only about twenty percent of women reliably have orgasm during unassisted coitus. This is not a very effective device for rewarding women to have sex with men.

Orgasm for women during unassisted coitus requires much longer (an average of twenty minutes) than orgasm by digital stimulation (an average of four minutes). Women who do not have orgasm during unassisted coitus are able to achieve orgasm by clitoral stimulation with the same success rate as other women. Also, women who achieve orgasm through clitoral stimulation or masturbation do so in the same time required by males to achieve orgasm in coitus or by masturbation, that is, in about four minutes. This means that women do not really take longer than men to have an orgasm. During masturbation, men and women require approximately the same amount of time to have an orgasm. Women take longer than men to have an orgasm only during heterosexual coitus. It seems that the orgasm may encourage women to have sex, <u>but not with men</u>.

Women who can form strong emotional bonds with other women have an additional option available when searching for assistance in raising their offspring. Human females need assistance in raising their young, but that assistance does not have to come from a male. In fact, males can be a danger to young children, especially children whom they did not father. One of the functions of the female orgasm may be to encourage human females to engage in sex not with males, but with other females. All evidence indicates that human females achieve orgasm more easily during masturbation than during sex with males. Perhaps the female orgasm is more important to homosexual sex than it is to heterosexual coitus. If so, it would be adaptive because it provides women with an alternative, safer means of obtaining the support they need during pregnancy and nursing. Intriguingly, this would mean that the occurrence of female orgasm during sex with males is just a side effect of its main purpose, which is related to sex with other females.

Also, consider the advantage enjoyed by those Paleolithic females who had a powerful tool for cementing social bonds between themselves exclusive of the males. In the primitive setting, a single male could dominate a single female, but a coalition of females could overpower an abusive or domineering male. This pattern has been well documented among female bonobos, who routinely use female homosexual sex to form coalitions. They then use those coalitions to dominate the males and control the social structure of the troop. I suspect that human females once did likewise.

One More Consideration

There was a time, during the Paleolithic, when sex among humans was not restricted by codes of conduct, laws, and religion. It may well be that, under primitive conditions of high promiscuity, nearly all females were orgasmic. Human females are selective about when and with whom they orgasm. If Laumann, et al., are correct and the average American female has only six sexual partners in a lifetime, then many women may simply not have experienced enough partners to find one with the precise combination of personality, coital pattern, and genital anatomy to induce orgasms. Maybe modern women have low rates of coital orgasm because modern cultures restrict their opportunities to sample enough lovers.

A Sense of Humor

God told men they would find faithful and obedient wives in all the corners of the Earth. Then men discovered that God had made the Earth round, and God laughed and laughed.

11

Finding Each Other

♦

I was looking for love in all the wrong places
Looking for love in too many faces

JOHNNY LEE

If you discover yourself alone and without a mate, how do you find one? Unless you live in rural North Dakota, people are all around you all the time. Most of those people are lonely too, so it should not be difficult to find someone to cuddle with. How do people locate and identify potential mates, screen them, and decide whom they want? Keep in mind that it has to be a mutual process. It is no good for person A to identify, locate, and choose person B, unless person B has also identified, located, and chosen person A. This is a tricky business. When a lot of other people are involved, as they always are, and when some of them are adversaries, as often occurs, things get downright confusing. Social networking is the process that sorts all this out. In much the same way that the forces in a moving stream of water sort out grains of sand into bands of similar composition, weight, and size, social networks bring together groups of people with enough common characteristics to cause adherence and formation of social bonds. People who are looking for mates must learn to let their social networks do the work for them.

The process of locating new mates is, in many ways, similar for both males and females, but the goals are different. Both sexes rely on their social networks to provide potential candidates and to perform filtering functions. Both sexes put their social capital at risk, in hopes of getting a good return on their investments. Both rely primarily on scripts when choosing mating strategies and making decisions.

The most difficult part of choosing a mate often lies in each person deciding what he or she wants. Most people simply do not know what they want. They are much better at identifying what they don't want. They have a vague template of an ideal mate, constructed from relationships with parents, the lessons of religion, traditional narratives, fairy tales, peer pressure, and television. People wander around, sampling each other, comparing them to the templates, and discarding the ones who do not match. For the most part, people are not aware of the templates, and simply do not know what they are seeking. However, both men and women do have certain genetically programmed desires, of which they are often unaware, or which they simply deny.

People want someone with whom they can be comfortable. They search for companionship and a hedge against loneliness and isolation. They also search for someone they can touch. They look for the pleasure of intimacy, ranging from simple closeness to frank sex.

Men instinctively search for both long-term and short-term mating opportunities, and have vastly different criteria for the two types of mates. For a man, a potential long-term mate is a woman with good parenting potential, a high degree of fidelity, social network compatibility, and the right attractiveness. A man instinctively looks for youth, good health, symmetric features, and the hourglass figure.

A potential short-term mate is almost any woman who is available for sex. For a human male, there is a potential evolutionary advantage to be gained from every opportunity for sex with any female. The emphasis is on availability, with only secondary concerns for attractiveness, health, and safety.

Women also instinctively search for both long-term and short-term mating opportunities, and their criteria are in some ways similar to, and in other ways different from those of men. A woman instinctively searches for a long-term mate who will be a good provider. She judges a man in terms of his employment (formally his hunting skills), resources, quality of clothing and automobile, and of his social rank among other men. She also looks for a man who can provide physical protection, and so prefers someone in good health and good physical shape.

In a long-term mate, a woman instinctively prefers a frugal man. She does not want someone who throws away resources that she may one day consider to be hers. This is in contrast to a woman's short-term strategy, in which she instinctively looks for a man who lets go of his money or resources easily. The primitive short-term strategy in a female is directed mostly toward obtaining resources -- a woman wants a man to spend money on her with few expectations in return.

Short-term mating instincts in the human female may have an alternative purpose. A woman who already has a long-term partner can obtain a higher quality of genetic material for her offspring from a short-term partner. This strategy compels her to search out discreet opportunistic couplings with highly attractive males during her time of fertility. She has an instinctive drive to aggressively pursue sex with a male of high physical attractiveness, bravado, or political power if she is in estrus and the proper opportunity arises.

That summarizes, in a very condensed fashion, the instincts that drive people in their search for mates, based on their genetic programming. Over the past fifty years, not to mention the last 5000, things have changed drastically. Ready availability of effective birth control and highly reliable latex condoms have made it possible for both men and women to seek out short-term partners just for pleasure, without any worry about pregnancy or disease. They have also made it possible for people to enter into informal intimate relationships, trying out candidates as new mates, without the risk of premature pregnancy. That is to say, they can just shack up together. With economic equality, women make decisions without regard to the earning power of potential mates. Sexual freedom for women allows men to obtain sexual partners at a much-reduced cost in terms of resources expended. None of that changes the genetic instructions that control reproductive behavior. It only sets people free to behave the way they did before they knew the connection between sex and pregnancy. People still have the same likes and dislikes today that they had in the Stone Age. Today they simply have a lot more leeway in how they choose to respond to those likes and dislikes.

Social Networks

Social networks act as filters to find potential mates. In early human pre-history, that may well have been their primary purpose. Your social network is the collection of all the people you know, and all the people they know, and all the people they know, etc. For mating purposes, it is everyone who is aware that you are available and searching for a mate.

Social networks have similarities to thermodynamic, electrical, and communication networks. There is a special branch of mathematics dedicated to the subject, and when applied to mating behavior, it is called social-network analysis. It is widely used in computerized matchmaking and other Internet applications. There is a category of Internet applications that allow users to join virtual social networks where they are linked to other users according to their relationships. A user can visualize her entire network as a web of points and lines. These Internet utilities are highly simplified. Real-life social networks are much more complicated and much less transparent.

Everyone has a social network. It can be broken down by the nature of the connections, that is, according to the context in which an individual knows the members of the network. Some members of one's social network may be people from work, and these may be current co-workers, ex-co-workers, and other work-related contacts, such as clients, vendors, and supervisors. Others might be members of one's family, or extended family, or in-laws, or ex-in-laws. Another category is the members of one's religious community, and all the people they know. School contributes classmates, acquaintances at school, teachers, ex-teachers, and alumni. The classmates of one's children, and the parents of those children, and the teachers at that school are all in one's social network, as are one's auto mechanic, grocer, and dentist, and all the people who work for them, and all their clients. All of a person's kin are included, as are all of their neighbors. Most people have primary social networks that contain hundreds or thousands of direct contacts, and each of these contacts has his own social network. It is not at all unreasonable to assume that the entire extended social network of an average sociable person contains tens of thousands of people.

Why, then, is it so difficult for an individual to find a mate among this many people? It is because the great majority of the people in the social network are not potential mates, due to age, sex, sexual preference, religion, social standing, social connection, attractiveness, or availability. There are so many exclusions. Humans do not date their own kin. Medical-care workers do not date their patients or family members of the patients. People generally prefer mates close to their own age range. Jews do not date Muslims. Highly educated women do not date uneducated men, and low-earning men do not attempt to woo high-earning women. The list goes on and on. The first task is to identify those few individuals who have some reasonable chance of being contenders. The good social network does this. It finds candidates, sorts them out, identifies potential mates, and brings them together.

Consider potential mates that come from one's social network in the following manners: Two people choose each other from among acquaintances that drink at the same bar. All they know about each other is that they are both lonely, and they both drink alcohol. That is not very promising. How about if they choose each other from among co-workers at the same place of employment? Well, at least they know they both have jobs. They also have some idea of each other's social standing and level of education.

When two people meet through their church activities, they have a lot more in common. They know each other's ethical frameworks, religious beliefs, and social standing in the community. They also share a very large part of their social networks, and many of their personal values. And they have fairly reliable information about each other.

How about if two people are introduced by their mothers? Chances are the information they receive about each other is based more on the mothers' wishes than on truth. It is not very reliable information. An introduction by one's sibling has greater potential to identify a possible mate. An introduction by a roommate is even better. Your roommate is most likely to know what you would like and dislike in a potential mate, and also knows your true habits and idiosyncrasies.

The social network filters potential mates through a process in which the members of the network make decisions on behalf of an individual. Friends and acquaintances decide who should and should not be encouraged. An individual who is actively searching for a mate makes the fact known to the social network. The members of the network then set about networking. Human beings are natural-born matchmakers.

Of course, there will be a great deal of disagreement within the network. Rarely does full consensus occur. Members have competing goals, and individuals may have hidden agendas. The network filtering process is muddled by jealousy, spite, and intrigue. Ultimately, in a free society, an individual seeking a mate must make decisions for herself.

But that is not true in all cultures. Historically, over the past five thousand years, most marriages have been arranged, even in the Judeo-Christian cultures. Recall that this was the theme of *Fiddler on the Roof*. Tradition among Russian Jews dictated that a matchmaker in the community chooses mates for young people, and without tradition people would be as precarious as a fiddler on the roof.

Some societies and cultures today still allow mating decisions to be made entirely by members of the social network. Most Hindu marriages are arranged, and many Hindu couples do not meet each other until the wedding day. In Hindu cultures, the social network makes all of the mating decisions. The wedding participants have no input whatsoever. Acquaintances and family members perform all searches and selections. In conservative Muslim societies, women are confined to residences, and have no opportunity to find or choose mates. Prospective mates are chosen for them by their social network. Because of their confinement, their social networks are limited to relatives and acquaintances of relatives. However, Muslim women, unlike their Hindu counterparts, do have some say in the decision. Sharia Law allows Muslim women to veto a proposed marriage. A Muslim woman and her male guardian must both approve of a potential husband before the marriage can take place.

The Economic Model

In Western societies, men and women are now free to make their own reproductive choices. They do not suffer the oppression (or enjoy the luxury) of proxy decision-makers. They must weigh the opportunities and the risks, and decide for themselves.

But how does one make such decisions? What does one take into consideration? One model of this decision-making process is based on economics and individual social capital.

Social capital is all those things projected onto you by your social network that determine the net value of your character. It can be viewed as a group of commodities. That is to say, you own your social capital. It consists of such things as your self-esteem, reputation, time, wealth, youth, beauty, health, personal safety, freedom, legal standing, earning potential, reproductive potential, social rank, and education. These are the things that you have to offer to a mate, and the things you put at risk when you invest in a relationship.

Every interaction that people have with their social networks requires some investment of social capital. It places some amount of capital at risk, and offers some promise of return on that investment. Inviting someone to lunch is an investment intended to enhance a social bond, but making the invitation risks a rejection and loss of self-esteem. Going out on a date is an investment of time and money, in hopes of building a relationship or enhancing one's social standing, but it places all that capital at risk if the date goes poorly. Proposing a new idea at work is notoriously risky business, with high potential for gain or loss.

A simple introduction and offer of a handshake involves the risk of rejection, or a botched name, or a flubbed handshake. Every man knows the risk of a self-introduction to a woman. An entire branch of informal social sciences is dedicated to the subject of "pick-up" lines, and the associated "get lost" responses. A Google search of "science of dating" + "pick-up lines" yields five thousand hits. Whole books are published on this one subject. It is all very anxiety provoking. One risks loss of self-esteem when using a pick-up line, but it is worth the risk if it leads to an opportunity to reproduce. Personal choices are often made based upon assessments of risk and benefit, but people are generally not aware of the economic nature of their decisions.

Both men and women are very aware of the appearance of the people they are seen with in public. Women want to show off a date who is "hot" while men like to be seen with "arm candy." Such public displays enhance their reputations and increase their social capital. The converse is true as well. A well-to-do woman is not going to want to be seen cuddling in public with a man who is dressed like a bum. A well-to-do man is not going to be pleased with his wife if she shows up at public function with unkempt hair and no makeup. Parents are certainly aware of this. They constantly worry about the company their children keep, and the effects on the reputations of their sons and daughters. Reputation is an important part of social capital. A bad reputation closes doors and severs connections in one's social network. The value of reputation as social capital is evident when people speak of "loss of reputation," as if it were a physical commodity.

Consider a woman who has been asked out on a first date by a man. She has to decide whether she will benefit from a relationship with him. If she invests of herself in this person, will she yield a return on that investment? Before she decides, she will need the answers to a long list of questions:

- What is his reputation, and will it enhance or tarnish hers?

- What is his potential as a long-term mate, based on earning power, education, and other factors?

- Would her wealth be enhanced by a long-term relationship with him?

- Does he have money, and is he willing to spend it on her?

- How physically attractive is he?

- Would she want to be seen in public with him?

- Would she want her children to resemble him?

- Is he fun to be with?

- Is he safe to be with? Does he have a history of violence, or criminal activity, or substance abuse? Would he cause her to end up in jail or to lose her earning potential?

- If she has children, how will he behave toward them? Will he accept them and father them, or will he be a risk to them?

- What are his intentions? Does he have a history of short-term relationships, just casual sex, or is he looking for a wife? This is especially pertinent if he is in her primary social network, where she may have to interact with him on a day-to-day basis.

All this must be determined before she ever gets the chance to find out if she likes him. The members of her social network will be her sources of information. They will answer most of these questions for her.

Of course, the information she gets may not be reliable. Some members of her social network may be her adversaries. It is not at all uncommon for women to give each other misleading information about eligible men. The most detrimental thing one woman will tell another about a man is that he overstates his financial situation or employment prospects, and she would have to support him. Members of her social network who are adversaries may also provide false information to the man, telling him that she sleeps around, or conversely, that she does not give sex, depending on what the informant thinks the man is looking for in this woman.

The rules of fair play do not apply in love and war.

John Lyly's, *Euphues* (1578).

The same is true for a man deciding whether to engage in or continue a relationship with a woman. He bases his initial decisions on information provided by his social network. He may solicit information from his male and female friends regarding her availability, and will receive unsolicited information as well. His mother will certainly have some input when she finds out about it!

Just as for women, much of the information a man receives may be unwelcome, unverifiable, or untrue. He may have adversaries who seek her attention, and she may have adversaries seeking him. The most detrimental charge against a woman is promiscuity, leading a man to believe that she will engage in infidelity. Other common derogatory assertions are that she stops giving sex after marriage, or that she wastes money or resources.

The economic model really says that every decision about relationships that is made on a logical basis takes into account a risk-benefit ratio. A person must consider the risk of a certain action, and the potential benefit. Assessments of both the risk and benefits may be based on faulty, or frankly false, information. Based on information provided by the social network and casual observation, each person must decide for himself or herself what to do next, whether to "sit it out or dance."

Scripting

When a person chooses a course of action in almost any situation, he or she relies on knowledge of how other humans have acted in that situation. Every person carries around a collection of memories gained from experience, observations, theater, movies, books, oral traditions, and religious teachings. This amounts to a huge repertoire of scripts for social behaviors in every conceivable situation. Social-scripting theory says that people choose from these scripts in deciding how to act. That is, they are acting out a part they have seen elsewhere. They are role-playing, following the examples set by their role models.

Human emotions are controlled by primitive instincts, which result from genetic programming, and they do not change from one generation to the next or from one culture to another. Human beings are, by nature, promiscuous, and every interaction is a potential mating opportunity. It is natural for a human male to scrutinize every female he meets as a possible alternative mate or opportunistic sexual partner. It is natural for a human female to consider every male in her environment to be a potential alternative long-term mate, or an opportunistic resource in raising her children, or an opportunity for an extra-pair coupling. These normal instinctive behaviors are left over from the Paleolithic Era, when it was beneficial to act upon such urges.

Some definitions of the verb "to act"

1. to do something; exert energy or force; be employed or operative.
2. to reach, make, or issue a decision on some matter.
3. to operate or function in a particular way.
4. to behave or conduct oneself in a particular fashion.
5. to pretend or feign.
6. to perform as an actor; to follow a script.
7. to represent a fictitious or historical character.
8. to feign or counterfeit an emotion
9. to behave as if having a certain character.

From Dictionary.com, the online dictionary.

Those urges, those primitive instincts are common to all members of the human species, but all humans do not act the same. Unlike lower animals, humans can choose how to act upon their instinctive urges. How they choose to act is determined by their upbringing, culture, and the repertoire of scripts they carry.

Scripts are extremely variable from one culture or generation to another, depending on a person's age, religion, legal climate, personal morals, and past experiences. Mating instincts are coded into the DNA, but humans do get to choose how they act on those instincts. They do so by choosing their scripts.

When an American woman dresses attractively, puts on her make up, and goes out to a bar to try to attract a male companion, she is following a script. She has arranged herself to attract the attention of males, inviting them to approach her. This gives her the opportunity to reject all but the one she chooses. It is as if she is wearing a T-shirt that says on the front, "Please love me," and on the back, "Not you, stupid."

When a Hindu newlywed couple, who have only met for the first time that day, engage in the first sex of their lives, with family members watching to ensure consummation of the deal, they are following a script, as are the observing family members. When a father gives away his daughter to the groom in a Christian wedding, all three are following a script. In fact, it is usually part of a play they have rehearsed the prior evening.

The couple that elopes against the wishes of their parents are also following a script. It is called, "We are young and in love, and that's all that matters." When a wealthy older man marries a younger single mother, and rescues her and her children from economic woes (and possibly from the consequences of her own bad decisions), he is following a script called, "The White Knight," and she is following a script called, "My Prince." Pickup lines that men and women use in bars, libraries, or wherever, are scripts. Rejection lines are also scripts. Both are rehearsed regularly. Here is a description of a standard Western dating script:

> "There are three possible parts to a date, of which at least two must be offered: entertainment, food, and affection. It is customary to begin a series of dates with a great deal of entertainment, a moderate amount of food, and the merest suggestion of affection. As the amount of affection increases, the entertainment can be reduced proportionately. When the affection *is* the entertainment, we no longer call it dating. Under no circumstances can the food be omitted." ~*Miss Manners' Guide to Excruciatingly Correct Behaviour* by Judith Martin

The rules of dating are scripts and vary in different cultures. In the Western urban culture, the standard script involves a male asking a female for a block of her time to attend an event with him, such as a dinner, concert, or party. He must ask her a minimum number of days in advance. Otherwise, he risks that she will not accept the offer, either because that block of her time is already promised to someone else, or because she will not admit that she does not already have a date for that evening. He pays their expenses for the evening and provides transportation.

On the initial date, they will go to a public place. They will both dress stylishly. They will talk about non-sexual matters, and engage in non-sexual touching. Subsequent dates will become gradually more intimate, until the couple find themselves in the script depicted in the first few paragraphs of chapter 10.

The modern world offers an endless variety of courting scripts, but most are variations on a few basic themes. The young lovers who defy their social networks and end in disaster are the same in *Pyramus and Thisbe, Romeo and Juliet, West Side Story,* and probably *The Graduate,* though the story ends prematurely. Damsels in distress have been rescued by their knights and princes since the beginning of time. Powerful men have fallen from grace under the influence of sensuous women and their own hormones from Helen of Troy to Monica Lewinski. Of course, the classic script everyone hopes to perform in the Western world is called "Happily ever after." The actors fall deeply in love, overcome all obstacles, and remain in romantic bliss until the end of time. But it is, after all, just a script, an act, a play. It is not real.

The acceptable scripts for modern dating in the Western culture can be found in a cornucopia of self-help books lining the shelves in Barnes and Nobles. The classic is *The Rules*, by Ellen Fein and Sherrie Schneider, which gives females the guidelines on how to find and snare Mr. Right. It is accompanied by a tongue-in-cheek male response entitled *The Code*, by Nate Penn and Lawrence LaRose, which tells males how to avoid being snared, while still getting sexual access to females. There are a thousand titles in between, from the beginner's *Dating for Dummies*, by Joy Browne, to the advanced *Guerilla Dating Tactics*, by Sharyn Wolf. These give the fine details of the scripts in an analytical fashion. But the basic form of the scripts comes from our religions, children's stories, movies, and romantic tales of adolescence.

Summary

This ends a very simplified explanation of how people find their mates, and indeed the process was simple at one time in human history. Humans are still genetically programmed for that time, but humans now live in a completely different environment. The changes started with the development of towns and cities, sped up with long-distance transportation, and went exponential with long distance communication. Humans are designed to interact face-to-face with at most a few thousands individuals, about the number of people in a tribe or a few villages. Today we are exposed to millions of people, mostly at a distance, via radio, television, telephone, the Internet, social networking, instant messaging, cell phones, and text messaging. It is not surprising that our basic instincts seem out of place.

People still find each other though, ferreting out a signal in all that cacophony of background noise. They still form couples and manage to spend enough time together to see if their ego boundaries collapse. They somehow learn enough about each other to determine if there is a script they can share. Then they try to stay on the same page together long enough to form a pair bond and make a life together, usually without ever considering why they do so.

12

An Alarming Novelty

Birth control is the first important step a woman must take toward the goal of her freedom. It is the first step she must take to be man's equal. It is the first step they must both take toward human emancipation.

MARGARET SANGER

A woman needs a man like a fish needs a bicycle.

IRMA DUNN

As the family goes, so goes the nation and so goes the whole world in which we live.

POPE JOHN PAUL II

The end of the human race will be that it will eventually die of civilization.

RALPH WALDO EMERSON

In the year 2525, if man is still alive, if woman can survive, they may find...

RICK EVANS OF ZAGER AND EVANS

The chapter title and the five quotes above are admittedly enigmatic. We, as a species, are in the midst of great turmoil. Recall the remark by Somerset Maugham that the purpose of falling in love is to trick people into having children. When reproduction is separated from the process of falling in love, it drastically alters the natural course of human history. The Law of Unintended Consequences states that "intervention in a complex system always creates unanticipated and often undesirable outcomes." Let us now consider some of the unintended consequences of the ongoing changes in human reproductive processes.

Over the past fifty years, women have regained much of the sexual freedom they had in the Paleolithic era, and men have regained sexual access to women without incurring long-term financial obligations. Contraception allows people to exercise their sexuality with a degree of freedom not seen since the Paleolithic Age, when people did not know or care about the consequences of sex.

Contraceptive technology has enabled the emergence of an entirely new class of humans. Their lifestyle has become so commonplace in the Western culture that it is no longer recognized as a novelty. A huge segment of the population is now free from the burdens of childrearing without sacrificing their sexuality. Hundreds of millions of people are now able to expend their life efforts on whatever they choose, whether it is the advancement of human culture and science, or simply the pursuits of leisure.

However, when women can support themselves and control their reproductive functions, marriage and the traditional two-parent family become marginalized. When birth control is adopted selectively by certain groups, this non-uniformity results in changes in the composition of the human gene pool.

When men and women are placed into close proximity to each other in the workplace, they must suppress their natural sexual behaviors. When the ratio of childless people to childrearing people increases drastically, it effectively dethrones the clergy, the sterile caste, who have historically provided moral guidance and leadership to the mass of the population making up the reproductive caste.

Look again at Dan and Alicia, who went through graduate school together as a couple and then went their separate ways in their professional lives. This would not have been possible as little as fifty years ago. Without birth control, they would have acquired children during their four years together, and those children would have constrained their professional and personal choices. Instead, they were both able to complete professional degrees, and they remained free to separate when their pair bond ended. An old adage says that "There is nothing new under the sun." But when two healthy, reproductively mature mammals form a pair with some purpose other than creating offspring, this is genuinely new in the animal kingdom. In fact, this is drastically, astoundingly, and perhaps catastrophically new, and the possible consequences warrant close scrutiny.

The Marginalization of Marriage

Like Dan and Alicia, the great majority of childless adults are in relationships but not married, simply because marriage has become superfluous. These are the childless-by-choice couples. Their existence has been made possible by technologies such as birth control, preventive medicine, civil engineering, and agriculture. Birth control allows them to have a sexual relationship without the burden of children. They live in a land of plenty, with good health and ample food. When free of disease, famine, and war, they are not compelled to produce ten children so that two might survive. They do not need children to help with work in the garden, on the farm, or in the family industry or business. They can put off having children, or choose not to have them at all.

Birth control and economic equality have given women freedom, or rather, given women <u>back</u> their freedom, to explore their sexuality. But there is a downside. When women can make themselves available to men without risk of pregnancy, men have access to casual sex with those women at a greatly reduced social cost to themselves. Increased sexual freedom for women is also increased sexual access for men, and consequently decreased sexual bargaining power for women. As the saying goes, "Why buy a cow, when you can get milk for free?" Female control over access to the womb has historically been women's source of financial power. For eons, women have been able to obtain resources and commitments from men in exchange for the opportunity to reproduce using the women's bodies.

Furthermore, many women are now self-sufficient, able to raise children without the support of a spouse. When women are able to go it alone, and so many are willing to do so, it becomes much more difficult for traditionally minded women to recruit and retain traditionally minded husbands who will support them and their children for the long term. The bargaining power granted to women by virtue of their possession of a womb is greatly reduced because they have been undersold by their competitors. The product they have to offer on the market has been devalued.

Add the Internet into the equation, and traditionally minded women don't stand a chance at securing mates in the old-fashioned way. There are eight billion web sites on the Internet, and four percent of them are pornographic. Each has thousands of images. There are more photos and videos of naked women on the Internet than there are women on Earth. For $19.95 a month, a man can buy access to more women than he could use in a hundred lifetimes. A chaste woman cannot compete with that many hussies.

The value of male sex, on the other hand, has always been zero because men are willing to give it away freely. Men lose nothing and gain a great deal when sex becomes more available to all. However, from a reproductive point of view, the sex that men obtain from women under the new rules is of greatly diminished value. Sex does not result in offspring when women use birth control, or when the women are electronic images on a computer screen. Men have more free access to women for sex, but not for reproductive services.

It has become more difficult for young men to reproduce simply because the young women are all using birth control. Women have always born the greatest share of the burden of childrearing, and are, therefore, the most incentivized to make the decision and take the necessary action to avoid pregnancy. Independent young women are, after all, independent, and make their own reproductive choices without regard to the desires of young men.

Men do bring services of their own to a relationship, but those have also been devalued. Men who want to raise a family have no leverage with which to obtain reproductive services from women who are financially independent and on birth control. Such women no longer have any need for the protection and provisions men once provided. Liberated women do not have to obligate themselves to a lifetime of childrearing in order to secure their futures. They simply do not need the services of a man enough to obligate themselves to bear and raise his children.

My friend Alexis is now twenty-seven and unmarried. She was once in love with a young man her age. They went through college together and then parted. When I first met her, years ago, she wanted to have six children. Now, she has no man in her life. She is well educated, sociable, pretty, and very bright. She seems like a woman who would have no trouble finding a mate. Alexis recently purchased her own home. She said it would be a nice place to raise children if she ever married. But she has not found anyone who interests her. It is difficult for a woman like Alexis to find a suitable mate, a man who would meet her emotional and intellectual needs and have higher earning power than she has. Alexis already has a home and an income. What would a man bring to their relationship? What would he have as a power base when they quarrel? He would have no way to hold on to her after their initial passion fades.

I suspect that Alexis has defaulted into a matrilineal life-style, in which she needs a male only to father her children. When a man comes into her life, he will come into her home only for the duration of the pair bond. They may not marry at all. When the romance fades, he will be left with no power base in the relationship. In time, he will leave and another man will replace him. As happens in primitive hoe-based agricultural societies, she will own the home and the children, and men will be transients.

This is the route that my junior colleague Caroline has now taken, too. As a professional, she can support herself and her child without the assistance of a mate. She is free to leave her husband and be independent. She will survive just fine as a single mother. She does not need to be subservient to a male in return for her support. If she chooses to have more children, she can choose another mate for that purpose.

Perhaps this is the underlying cause of the findings revealed in the 2006 National Vital Statistics Report. Over the past fifteen years, the percentage of children born out of wedlock has risen from twenty-nine percent to thirty-eight percent, despite the fact that the number of out-of-wedlock pregnancies among teenagers has decreased. The entire increase has been among women in the twenty- to forty-year-old age group who are having children out of wedlock by choice.

Many independent women simply do not feel that it is worth the trouble to have men in their lives, even after they have children. In our modern, urban, civilized society, there often is no place for men. A man to a woman really is like a bicycle to a fish. Any woman who has ever had to remove a snake from the bathroom, free up a farm tractor from four feet of mud, clear a fallen tree from the road, or gut and skin a steer quickly learns to appreciate the value of a man. There are unique times when men are indispensable. But now the Western world is civilized. The wolves, hyenas, and snakes are gone from suburbia. The roads and bridges are all built. Food comes from the local grocery store. What is there for a man to do in daily life that a woman cannot? The answer, of course, is that a man can impregnate a woman. An independent woman needs nothing else from the father of her child that she cannot obtain on her own, or from other women.

This is a drastic change from one hundred years ago. Women needed men for support. And when women needed men, they had sex with men and they ended up having babies. But when women are independent of men, they have fewer offspring, just because they are less obligated to have sex. Bright, independent young women have fewer offspring than dependent women. They have lower reproductive success.

The Law of Unintended Consequences
An Illustration

All unwed pregnant women in the U.S. are automatically eligible for Medicaid benefits. The government will pay all the costs of the pregnancy, delivery, and post-partum care for an unmarried woman. As a result, it has become commonplace for uninsured couples to delay marriage until after they have a family.

But this behavior is not restricted to the poor. A local well-to-do attorney and business owner delayed marrying his live-in girlfriend until she delivered their second child. It was a simple business decision. Her medical bills were covered by tax dollars.

She is now among those women counted on the census as unwed mothers. The increased rate of childbirth to unwed mothers in their twenties and thirties is in part due to financial incentives from the government.

An Interesting Encounter with Two Women

Connie, a twenty-six year old white female, came to my ER with low abdominal pain, which started during the night after she used intravenous crystal meth. Crystal meth does not generally cause abdominal pain, so I considered what else might have caused the patient's pain. Mostly, I thought about what she might have done to pay for the drugs she had consumed during the night. I asked one of my female ER techs, Vicky, to come with me as a chaperone while I interviewed and examined the patient. Vicky is a twenty-nine-year-old white female, a nursing student, and a professional secretary for the ER.

When I entered the exam room, I was surprised by how much the two women looked alike. They were both attractive and fresh looking, with good complexions, symmetric features, and oval faces. They looked like healthy, pretty, farm girls.

I questioned the patient about her symptoms and about the circumstances of her drug use. She had broad lower abdominal pain and it hurt when she walked. She denied any pain with urination. She thought she might have a vaginal discharge. She had no nausea or vomiting. Her menses had been normal. She had recently been told by a physician that she had a urinary tract infection, and was given antibiotics and pain pills. She did not take the antibiotics, although she did take the pain pills.

She admitted that she was unemployed and had no means of supporting herself. She had to "hustle" the drugs wherever she could. She admitted to prostitution in the past, but claimed that she had not done so in the last month. She admitted that she did not have any money to pay for the drugs she had used during the night. She said she could not remember if she had had sex during the night, but that if she did, it was "non-consensual."

On examination she had no abdominal tenderness. She also had no vaginal discharge and no internal tenderness on pelvic exam. There were no wounds or bruises on her genitalia to indicate rape. Her urinalysis and pregnancy test were normal. I did not find any infection. I gave her a prescription for some mild pain pills and discharged her.

During the exam, I noticed that the patient had extensive stretch marks and a relatively flaccid anterior abdominal wall from previous pregnancies. Afterward, I mentioned the patient's stretch marks to Vicky, and asked if she had thought about where the patient's children might be. Vicky said that she had actually asked the patient that question. There were three children. One of them had been taken by the state, one was in the custody of the maternal grandmother, and one was in the custody of the father.

This was an intriguing encounter. One of these women is twenty-nine, unmarried, well educated, gainfully employed, and childless. The other is twenty-six, also unmarried, and is an unemployed, drug-addicted prostitute, and the mother of three children who are being raised by other people. This begs a crucial question. From a biological perspective, which of these two women is better adapted to her environment? Or, to ask it another way, which of them will leave behind more surviving offspring and has had more reproductive success? The answer, of course, is the drug-addict prostitute.

Young people in the Western world today, if they are smart and responsible, can escape the burdens of childrearing. The example above compares two women, but the phenomenon is not limited to women. It is simply easier to demonstrate in women, because parenthood is unambiguous in females. Several childless men work with me, and each of them probably has less reproductive success than the fathers of this patient's three children. I say probably because it is difficult to know how many offspring a particular human male might have. But among human females, the determination can be made usually by counting on the fingers. The point I wish to make is that bright, talented, well-educated people are often less well adapted than their counterparts when measured in biological terms such as reproductive success.

It would have been unimaginable to people a hundred years ago that a women outside the confines of a convent would ever willingly choose not to bear children. Barren women were burned as witches or cast out of villages and towns. Even today, in the primitive places of the world, a barren woman is an evil thing, and her evil can infect other women. Such women are banished. Their bodies are buried in remote, unmarked graves. Even women who have borne children, but have suffered the death of all their children are ostracized. Fecundity was, and in some places still is, a woman's only value. In the Western cultures, that has all changed now, but the change did not occur very long ago.

About forty years ago, a paradigm shift occurred in the Western world, coinciding with the broadcast of *The Mary Tyler Moore Show*. This aired in the 1970s in the United States, and was ultimately very popular among the general viewers. However, it was initially highly controversial, and almost did not air. The focus groups that evaluated the show prior to airing did not approve of the concept and were offended by the morals of the main character, Mary Richards. She was a young, single woman pursuing a career in TV news broadcasting, instead of pursuing a husband. She had no ambition to marry or to bear children, and no inclination to live off the resources provided by a man. This was the first mainstream public woman allowed to lead the lifestyle previously monopolized by men. It was only forty years ago that the mindset of the United States underwent the paradigm shift to economic and personal freedom for women. Mary Richards did not earn her keep via reproductive services, and yet the general public embraced her character, if somewhat hesitantly. The *Mary Tyler Moore Show* marked a milestone in the social development of humanity. Ironically, Ms. Moore spent five years playing the role of the traditional housewife and mother, Laura Petri, on the *Dick van Dyke Show*, before taking on the role of the independently minded Mary Richards,

People choose to limit or forego reproduction for many different reasons, some of which are admirable and some perhaps not, but they are all valid. Some people prefer to devote their lives to other things: the betterment of the human condition, the development of a blue rose, the cure for cancer, saving the whales, or one of a million other causes. Others think that too many people exist in the world already. Some simply feel they would be lousy parents, and who can disagree with them? Others say they are too selfish for children, and they would rather retire early and sample fine cuisines around the world.

There are people who have spent their childhoods raising ten younger siblings, and feel as though they have already done their duty to humanity. Others would rather dote on their nieces and nephews at their leisure, then go back to their own peaceful homes and read a good book, or write one. Some people have deleterious genes, such as sickle cell disease or Huntington's chorea, which they would rather not inflict on their own children or future generations. For whatever reason, many couples are composed of individuals who choose to subvert their reproductive instincts and surrender their places in the gene pool.

I had a pleasant conversation one day with a young woman named Margaret, a waitress in a restaurant where I was eating dinner with my wife and young children many years ago. Margaret was very adept at entertaining our kids. I asked her if she had children of her own, and she said that she would never have any. She had helped raise her eight younger siblings, and she had had quite enough of childrearing. She had decided instead to go to college and become an attorney. Margaret represents that group of people who feel that they have done their share of the work of advancing humanity by raising their siblings, and have no need, desire, or obligation to have children of their own. They are like the worker ants who invest in their siblings, rather than their own offspring. This option would not have been easily available to Margaret prior to about 1960.

Jane was a strikingly beautiful young woman in my high school class. A tall Scandinavian blonde with a flirtatious personality, she was always surrounded by hopeful young men. At the thirtieth class reunion, she was still beautiful. She had never married, and she had never had children. She enjoyed her good looks and her suitors too much. Jane chose not to have children simply because she was unwilling to give up the lifestyle of one who is single and highly attractive.

Ann and Dennis are childless by choice. He has a hereditary disorder called epidermal dysplasia that causes abnormalities of skin, hair, and teeth. He does not want to transmit this disorder to children. And she prefers to teach and study instead of raising kids. So they married with the understanding that they would not have children. They both have doctorate degrees in the biological sciences, and are well-respected instructors and researchers at a university.

A young woman named Diane came into the ER one night with lower abdominal pain. She was a pretty coed from the local college, and her roommate, another nice young lady, had come along for moral support. As I was interviewing her, I asked her all those questions that one usually asks of a young woman with abdomen pain. When I asked her whether she might be pregnant, she responded, "No. I don't think so." Then she turned to her roommate, and said, "Your dad has had a vasectomy, hasn't he?" The roommate assured her that he had.

Diane is a great example of a young woman choosing an opportunistic short-term sexual partner. Modern birth control has freed this young woman to pursue her sexuality at liberty. When she has the urge to have sex, she finds a convenient, safe partner in her roommate's father. As an older man, he is probably a more competent lover than men her own age. The sex is not complicated by any potential for long-term obligations. He is also probably generous to her. And apparently she has the complete approval of her roommate, who is an essential part of her social network.

Birth control and economic equality have liberated Vicky, Margaret, Jane, Ann, and Diane to lead active, full lives, including sexual relationships, without creating offspring. In the process they forego the opportunity to propagate their genes. Of course, they are not alone. Each of them has men in their lives who have sexual access to these women without risk of the women becoming pregnant. Those men also forego the opportunity to create offspring and to propagate their genes. Their genes are also lost from the gene pool.

So, how can cultures survive when their best and brightest people opt out of reproduction? Well, we don't know that they do. The option to forego reproduction has only been available on a large scale for half a century. The concept may yet prove to be non-viable. The jury is still out on the matter. However, there must be some advantage that is offered to such a society or culture that offsets the loss of these individuals from the gene pool. That advantage arises from the services these non-reproducers provide in the workplace. Whether they will generate enough benefit to society to offset their loss from the gene pool is not yet known.

Idiocracy

Released in 2006 without fanfare, this movie has acquired a cult following. It is a science-fiction comedy that follows the adventures of two thoroughly average people who are moved forward in time 500 years. They find themselves in a world where the population has been so dumbed-down by lop-sided breeding that humanity has become profoundly stupid. The two protagonists are brilliant by comparison, the smartest people in the world, and it falls to them to save the human race from certain disaster.

Sexuality in the Workplace

In a culture that endorses sexual equality, men and women work side by side, and have equal social standing. This generates a whole new set of problems, by introducing sexuality into the workplace. When human males and females are in such close proximity, it is their nature to interact according to their genetic programming, i.e., sexually. However, there is a body of law that specifically prohibits any sexual behaviors in the workplace. It is intended to force people to interact in a purely professional manner. Federal regulations forbid such things as touching above the elbow, referencing any body parts in conversations, and discussing sexuality or reproductive functions. It is no longer simply being forward to compliment a woman on her figure, place a hand on her waist, or ask if she is pregnant. It is illegal. Off-color jokes and sexual chatter are no longer just in bad taste; they are violations of federal law. That such laws exist merely illustrates how difficult it is for people to suppress their sexual behaviors.

These workplace regulations are only marginally effective. Co-workers hug each other. Women talk about their pregnancies and labor experiences. Men complain about their wives and girlfriends. People share their concerns about health and discuss their bodily ailments. They compare their Kama Sutra applications on their iPhones. They discuss intimate details of their personal relationships. Sexual chatter, innuendo, and off-color jokes are ubiquitous. Inter-office and workplace romances are commonplace. On-the-job sex is one of the staples of office gossip.

Work is a very big part of a people's lives, both in terms of the portion of the social network represented by co-workers, and in terms of the time spent in the workplace. Humans are not going to exclude sexuality from such a large part of their existence. Suppression of sexuality requires defiance of one's genetic programming, and is not an easy thing to do. Too many opportunities and prospects would be missed. It

The Maid Gets a Raise

The maid asked for a raise.
The Madam was very upset, and asked, "Now Maria, why do you think you deserve a raise?"
"Well, Madam," she answered, "there are three reasons. The first is that I iron better than you do."
Madam asked, "Who said you iron better than I do?"
Maria answered, "The Master said so."
Madam said, "Oh,"
The maid said, "The second reason is that I cook better than you do."
"Nonsense!" said the Madam. "Who told you that you cook better than I do?"
"The Master did." answered the maid.
Madam responded, "Oh."
Maria went on, "And the third reason is that I am a better lover than you."
The Madam, now very upset, asked, "And did the Master say this as well?"
The maid answered, "No Madam, the gardener did."
The maid got a raise.

It is funny because it is plausible, and it is only plausible because sexuality permeates all aspects of human life, including the workplace. In this case, both the maid and the Madam have been having sex with the gardener. The gardener told the maid about the Madam's indiscretion, and now the Madam is screwed.

is virtually impossible to eliminate sexual behavior from any environment where humans congregate. Work is where most people recruit new mates. Popular magazines are filled with articles advising readers how to acquire the romantic interests of their co-workers.

Mating behavior is instinctive to humans, who continuously reconnoiter for alternative mates. Scouting requires probing others to determine their interests and receptivity. The probing is visual, verbal, and tactile. Body language, flirtatious comments, and casual touching are all parts of the process, and such intrinsic human behaviors will never be entirely eliminated from any place where people gather, including the workplace. It is unlikely that there exists a single workplace employing more than a dozen people that does not have frequent violations.

I overheard a conversation one morning at work in which a female respiratory therapist was talking casually with three male nurses outside my office door. She was telling them, "I finally found a sports bra like we talked about. One with, you know, 'coverage' when it gets cold out." This pretty, young woman had been having a running discussion with these three young men about the size of her nipples, the problems they cause when she exercises in cold weather, and her ongoing search for a bra that hides her nipple erections. It is tempting to discount this particular conversation as an innocent discussion of the technical design of undergarments. However, there is no doubt that this young woman's comments were titillating to the three young men, and that she knew why she had their attention. They have absolutely zero interest in the technical design of bras. She was talking about her nipples and they were listening intently. She was using her sexuality to get their attention.

Even in the absence of reproductive interests, sexual banter is rampant at work. Reproduction is an important part of life, and people talk about it. The highest incidence occurs in medical facilities and police stations, where no one is shocked by anything, and every facet of human behavior is fair game for casual conversation.

Nonetheless, casual conversations about sexual matters can be pretty annoying to some people, and they get offended and complain. Such complaints have to be acknowledged and acted upon. There has to be some oversight and regulation of sexuality in the workplace. Mating behaviors must be suppressed in work environments or nothing would ever get done. Sexuality is too distracting, and the workplace is too complicated. Power differentials and privileged information give individuals unfair advantages over one another. Superiors at work have the power to make decisions that impact their subordinates financially. On the other hand, subordinates have access to information that can have financial and social impact on their superiors. Workplace romances almost invariably generate conflicts that have negative impacts on productivity.

Unfortunately, the regulations regarding such behavior are often Draconian. They apply very harsh penalties and classify any suspected offenders as psychopaths and predators. For the most part, people want to engage in natural human behavior, and want to interact with each other on some sexual level. As a result, the general population does not "buy in" to the spirit of the regulations. Most people do not complain about sexual behavior among co-workers because they are not willing to be responsible for the harsh punishment meted out. Also, they do not want to call attention to their own workplace for fear of strict application of the regulations to themselves and their other co-workers. In the workplace, and elsewhere, male and female relationships are rarely completely fraternal. Men and women continuously assess each other as potential sexual partners. Wherever sexually mature human males and females come into social contact, this behavior will occur. Legislation cannot alter human nature.

Dethroning the Sterile Caste

Recall Ann and Dennis, the couple who chose to teach and engage in biological research rather than raise a family. Richard Dawkins, author of *The Selfish Gene*, would say that Ann and Dennis have chosen to concentrate on the perpetuation of their memes, at the expense of the perpetuation of their genes. Just as prime numbers are the building blocks of the number system, and genes are the building blocks of heredity, memes are the building blocks of cultures. Memes are the individual ideas, the distinct but intertwined concepts that make up a culture. Virginity at marriage is a meme. Each of the Ten Commandments is a meme. Einstein's famous formula, $E = mc^2$, is a meme. That people should be governed by the consent of the governed is a meme. The concept of a meme is in itself a meme, one created by Richard Dawkins.

People who write books, engage in research, or teach are propagating memes. People who proselytize or preach religion are also propagating memes. The non-sectarian teachers of scientific memes and the sectarian propagators of religious memes are historically in conflict. Over the past one hundred years, the number of people propagating memes in non-sectarian forums has increased exponentially. They have over-run the universities, schools, publishing houses, libraries, radio, television, and the Internet. They have smothered the churches, monasteries, and convents. The scientists, engineers, scholars, and philosophers now far outnumber the priests and proselytizers.

Since the beginning of recorded time, childless-by-choice was the privilege of the members of the clergy. Religious institutions were the only storehouses of knowledge, and were the powerhouses for advancement of philosophy, science, and art. Archimedes and his followers were sworn to celibacy. The great scientific minds of the renaissance belonged to priests. Nicolaus Copernicus, Galileo Galilei, Johannes Kepler, Isaac Newton, and Gregory Mendel were members of the clergy, and had no legitimate families. They lived and studied in places that were devoid of the distractions of child-drearing. They had no parenting duties. They were the sterile caste. This is why religious institutions were able to maintain a workforce that was free to copy textbooks, read existing literature, plant gardens of peas, and sort the F1 and F2 generations by color, time the speed of pendulums, invent the calculus, count the stars, and calculate the trajectories of planets. Their workers did not have to raise kids.

Virtually all of the advancements of science in the past five thousand years and up to about two hundred years ago occurred in religious institutions and under the supervision of religious leaders. But, since the Industrial Revolution, there has been a growing schism between the church and the universities. Over the last two centuries, first industry and then government started investing in science and research, independent of the church. As they did so, they intruded upon the territory of religious institutions, which had previously enjoyed a monopoly on natural philosophy.

The conflict has been there since ancient times. It became an insurgency when science and the church began to diverge in the Age of Enlightenment. The conflict between church and science, between religious teachings and non-sectarian teachings, still persists today, and the political power is balanced between the two factions. The Roman Catholic Church convicted Galileo of heresy in 1632 for stating that the Earth moved around the sun. Galileo's interpretations were shown to be correct prior to his death in 1664, but he was not pardoned by the Pope until 1992. In U.S. classrooms today, Intelligent Design has squared off against Evolution in a battle to be the dominant dogma of man's origin. As with the prosecution of Galileo, this is not a scientific debate about the relative merits of two theories. It is another skirmish in the ongoing war over a fundamental social question: Who will be in command of the collective human intellect? Religious institutions are vying with public educational systems over the control of the reins of human philosophy. Religion would base reality upon scripture, while science supports a version based upon logic. More importantly, and this is the heart of the matter, religion would provide moral guidance that comes from a higher power, while science would provide leadership that comes from human knowledge.

The same question is at the heart of the great schism in the house of Islam. A war rages all over the world right now that began with the writings of Taqi ad-Din Ahmad ibn Taymiyyah (1263–1338). He rejected any innovation, calling it a cursed intrusion of Christianity upon the true religion. Taymiyyah was Sunni. He declared that the laws of the universe were fixed as written in the Koran and should not be further investigated. He rejected the Shiite branch of Islam and declared jihad upon Shiites, because the Shiites accepted innovation and modernization of the laws by which men live. The Sunnis have difficulty accepting innovation and modernization, in part because it would require some drastic changes in the way men control their women. The Iranian Imams, the Taliban, and the Whahabi are all followers of the writings of Taymiyyah, who, incidentally, was Osama Bin Laden's hero and role model.

Until a few hundred years ago, it was obvious who controlled philosophy. There was no contest. Religious institutions had a monopoly on the workforce of childless adults. Churches owned the sterile caste. All science was controlled by religious entities, all academics answered to the church, and all libraries were owned by the churches and monasteries. This is no longer true.

Today, there is a vast army of people who are relatively free from the burdens of reproduction and childrearing, and yet are not in the service of any religious institution. They are the students, post-grads, researchers, and professors in public institutions around the world, plus all the researchers in public research facilities and government agencies, plus all the scientists employed in R&D in the private sector, plus all the physicians and learned professionals.

The number of people who pursue scientific and philosophical truth as a full-time profession has increased from a few thousand in the time of Galileo to hundreds of millions today, and virtually all of them today are free from the ideological intrusions of religion. The astounding leap forward of scientific knowledge over the past half century has been primarily due to the ready availability of birth control. This massive shift of human resources to the study of science has created a huge body of knowledge that threatens religion.

Is this transition sustainable? Can humanity survive changes this drastic and abrupt? When knowledge supersedes religion, there are unanticipated, undesirable effects. We humans have many needs that religion fills. There are reasons that gods persist in our scientific world. Robert A. Hinde, in *Why Gods Persist*, explains this in great detail. We need to feel in control, to have the company of another, and to not be alone. We need to understand the causes of adversity, to find shelter in a parent figure, and to ward off the fear of death. We need social structure, moral guidance, and a sense of purpose. Religion provides all this. Science cannot.

There is a much wider concern, though. What happens to a society that openly challenges religion? When too large a portion of the population substitutes scientific knowledge for faith, when science goes too far, when religion is driven back too much, the results may well be disastrous. The Soviet Union embraced the philosophy that religion is the opiate of the masses and tried to ban the churches. That effort failed miserably. The Soviet government could never get the people to buy into the idea of the state as an alternative to their gods. People need their gods. No matter how grandiose their intentions, the intelligentsia cannot win the hearts of the masses. The great majority of humanity cannot conceive of the reality that the intelligentsia purvey. They can only assimilate the simple narratives of religion.

The intelligentsia must be cautious. They must not push their agendas too hard. In *The God Delusion,* Richard Dawkins pushes too hard. He goes too far. His arguments against religion may be sound, but his frontal attack is doomed to failure. He fails to recognize that mere mortal humans need their gods. Humans have embraced gods since the beginning of time. There is a deeply rooted need in man for an omniscient and omnipresent parent. Humans fear an empty universe. Loneliness is a terrible demon. When non-sectarian knowledge goes too far and challenges the gods, people get angry.

They do strange things, terrible things. They commit religious genocide, slaughtering opposing groups. They take over airplanes and fly them into tall buildings. Mobs form and kill off the intelligentsia. They burn the libraries. The dark ages return.

The Library of Alexandria in Egypt was burned repeatedly, once by pagan mobs, once by Muslim hoards, and again by Christian mobs. The Inquisition was undertaken solely for the purpose of eradicating opposing scientific and religious ideology. Libraries and books were torched by the Brown Shirts in Germany, in a prelude to burning the bodies of the murdered Jewish intelligentsia. As recently as August 25, 1992, two ancient, irreplaceable libraries in Sarajevo were shelled with incendiary bombs. They were intentionally burned to the ground in a religious war. (Incidentally, that was the same year that Galileo was pardoned.) People become unimaginably destructive when their gods are threatened.

Today, those most educated are the least likely to be religious, as has been shown repeatedly, most recently in a Pew Research Center study published on September 28, 2010. The corollary is that those least educated are the most faithful. In a test of knowledge about the Christian religion, those who scored highest were the atheists and agnostics.

Only a week earlier, Pope Benedict spoke to the British parliament and advised that religion must not be allowed to become "marginalized" in the lives of the people. He warned that public policy must be governed by "moral principles," rather than by "nothing more solid than social consensus." What he was saying is that morality cannot be replaced by reason. It does not matter who is technically right and who is wrong in the debate of science against faith. It only matters which philosophy best meets the needs of the people, which provides the best moral guidance. This is sound advice. It must be heeded by the social architects who would revise our cultures based on science. It was a lesson learned the hard way by the Soviets, by Galileo, and by countless librarians from Alexandria to Sarajevo.

Humans are more compliant with rules that come from a higher power than they are with regulations written by the intelligentsia. That is the strength of religion. The intelligentsia may be the strength of a modern nation. They are the educators, engineers, political leaders, and scientists who are the heart of modernity. But the intelligentsia are mere humans, and have their own faults and weakness. The cultures that best utilize their intelligentsia to serve the needs of the people will ultimately supercede all others. Over the past three thousand years the clear winners in this competition have been the five great religions.

Summary

When humans developed agriculture, it catapulted humanity out of the Stone Age by enabling the development of specialized craftsmen, and the subsequent commerce of their goods. It freed the hands of people from the tasks of growing or gathering their food and allowed technological pursuits. During my lifetime, humans in the Western world have been freed from the burden of reproduction as well, and there has been a 10,000-fold increase in the number of humans available to advance technology. A thousand years from now, historians will identify this moment in time as a critical transition in human history. It is at this point that humans finally distinguished themselves from the animals and became so successful that they could forego reproduction and turn to other pursuits. Humans have seized control of their reproductive processes, and that achievement has enabled all of the other scientific advances of the past half century.

It is beyond my ability to say where all this change in reproductive behaviors will lead. But I can say that we are currently witnessing the greatest revolution in human culture since the invention of agriculture. Much of the conflict we see in the news each day is simply the convulsions of a species in cultural upheaval caused by changes in our reproductive behaviors. Reproduction is the core of our existence. It is hardwired into our genetics. It cannot be easily cast aside. Any change in the rules of reproduction will have far-reaching consequences. Most human behavior, from a young man's clothing choices for the day, to major political decisions resulting in international warfare, is impacted by our reproductive strategies.

The door has now been opened to a new age for Humanity. If we are to survive this transition, each of us must learn to live in harmony with our own emotions and sexuality. We need to develop a better understanding of our genetic programming, and a more realistic comprehensive model of human reproductive strategies.

13

The Mathematics of Sexual Preference

The world is not divided into sheep and goats. Not all things are black nor all things white. It is a fundamental of taxonomy that nature rarely deals with discrete categories. Only the human mind invents categories and tries to force facts into separated pigeon-holes. The living world is a continuum in each and every one of its aspects. The sooner we learn this concerning sexual behavior the sooner we shall reach a sound understanding of the realities of sex.

ALFRED KINSEY

Humans are highly versatile. They do not separate neatly into binary groups. The arbitrary assignment of individuals into categories such as male/female, masculine/feminine, or heterosexual/homosexual necessarily disenfranchises that part of the population who are the in-betweens and the others. Physiologic systems do not classify by morality. Human sexuality is a physiologic issue and not a moral one. Sexual diversity is just that -- diversity -- which arises from statistical variations in the anatomy, physiology, and psychology of sexuality. As such, it adds to the overall adaptability of human beings. Like any other characteristics of a population, sexual diversity would not be present unless it served some adaptive function. Humans would not be designed this way without a good reason.

Discussions of sexual diversity typically begin with homosexuality, so I will start there and show that homosexuality is a statistical result of human sexual variability. It occurs simply by chance. More importantly, it persists in the human population because, contrary to common beliefs, homosexuals are effective reproducers. Most people who engage in homosexual behavior are actually bisexual and are simply practicing reproductive strategies that defy the standard heterosexual paradigm. Homosexual behaviors are common in animals other than humans, and have been present in humans since prehistoric times. There is no logical basis for classifying such behaviors as unnatural.

Homosexuality is surprisingly common in humans and takes many different forms. To illustrate the point, here are some examples of people who have engaged in homosexual behavior at some time in their lives. These are either people who I have known personally, or people who are well known in the public eye. For the most part, they are upstanding citizens with careers, homes, and families. They are simply people who do not fit the standard heterosexual paradigm.

Karen is a tall, pretty, athletic brunette whom I have known for years. She was exclusively lesbian in high school. In college, she gradually assumed a bisexual lifestyle, which she continued into her professional life. She eventually married a successful attorney, becoming his younger second wife, his trophy wife. She had two children by him before he died in an auto accident. She went on to marry another professional man and to have two children by him.

Karen illustrates the flexibility that some people have in their sexual orientation. She demonstrates the phenomenon of age-related shifts in orientation. Many people change sexual orientation as they grow older. Karen also demonstrates the reproductive potential of women who are lesbians at some time in their lives. Here is a bisexual female who bore four children to two financially successful husbands. She and her lovely, happy family are seen in church every Sunday.

Sean was an elderly professional man when I knew him. He was still working at well past retirement age, mostly because his skills were needed in the community. He was a notorious homosexual, having been involved in a number of public scandals. His ex-wife was just as notorious for her bad temper and poor judgment. The two of them had three children together before she caught him in bed with another man and divorced him with a great deal of public drama.

This man was, at least publicly, heterosexual in early adulthood. That may be in part due to his age. He was young at a time when homosexuals were aggressively persecuted. After a few decades of marriage and three children, his pair bond with his wife had thoroughly expired. She not only divorced him, but she responded with contempt and publicly humiliated him.

After their divorce, the publicity surrounding his affair labeled him, and he adopted an exclusively homosexual lifestyle. This may also have been a change related to his aging, or it may have simply been due to ostracism. Clearly, Sean is not exclusively homosexual, but rather bisexual, and he is an effective reproducer. He has children and grandchildren.

Brian worked as an orderly in a local hospital for three decades, and was a valued employee. He was well liked by his patients, co-workers, and superiors. He never married and never shared anything about his private life with anyone. When he died suddenly of natural causes, one man in the community came forward to cry at his funeral, claiming to have been his lifelong lover.

Most homosexual people are good, solid members of the community. They just happen, by chance, to fall into that part of the bell curve that is across the centerline. They privately, quietly live their lives, playing the game with the cards that were dealt to them. The great majority of homosexuals and bisexuals are not out marching in parades or cross-dressing in public, calling attention to themselves. They are going about their lives, working at their jobs, paying their mortgages, and often raising their children just like everybody else.

Devin came to me in the ER one night depressed and feeling suicidal. It was the old story of a lover's triangle. Devin's girlfriend was sleeping with Devin's best friend. In this case, though, Devin, the girlfriend, and the best friend were all female. Homosexuals fall in love and fall out of love in the same way that heterosexuals do. They have the same temptations, the same betrayals, and the same drama and intrigue.

Late one evening, one of my nurses, a woman named Anne, told me the story of her first marriage. She was twenty-one, and David was two years older. Church was the center of their lives. They met there and continued attending regularly while courting and after marriage. The courtship lasted a year, and they remained married for a year. Although they had no children, they seemed to have a perfect marriage.

Anne told me how she came home one day to find her devoted husband sitting at the dining room table, crying, with a bottle of whiskey, two glasses, and a tape recorder. Neither of them were drinkers, but he poured some whiskey for each of them and played the tape. The message was from him to her, explaining that he loved her dearly and thought the world of her. He had tried very hard to be what she, his family, and God wanted him to be. But he was gay. He was totally miserable, living a complete lie, and could not go on this way.

They annulled the marriage. He left their hometown and moved to a large city. Anne was devastated. She was left confused about men, sexuality, and relationships. She was very pretty and had no trouble attracting new partners, but she went through a series of troubled marriages.

This couple illustrates so well the degree of influence that culture and family bring to bear on an individual's perceived sexual role. These two lovers were following a classic script of Christian romance, and it was completely wrong for them. He was acting out the part of a straight male and a loving husband, but it was just acting. She was acting out the part of a loving wife, completely ignoring whatever signs may have been present indicating a serious defect in their sex life.

This young man also exemplifies the confusion that bisexuals face in restrictive societies. He was able to function in a heterosexual relationship for two years, but remained miserable. He genuinely cared for the feelings of this woman, and he probably did love her, but his physical attraction to males was so much stronger that he was compelled to leave this attractive woman and face disgrace in his church, community, and family. He ultimately abandoned his entire social network to seek out a new life elsewhere.

Any discussion of homosexuality becomes mired in linguistics from the onset. Just deciding what constitutes a homosexual is problematic. Both males and females change their preferences over time in response to internal and external influences. There is no conclusive data as to how many people are homosexual, partly because the answer is dependent on time, place, and circumstances. If you count only those people who identify themselves as homosexuals, then about four percent of men and two percent of women are homosexual. If you count all those people who have ever had a sexual encounter with a member of their own sex, then the figures are ten percent and five percent respectively. However, if you include everyone who has ever been aroused by the thought of a member of their own sex, then the figure is as high as forty percent for both sexes. What is clear is that humans are highly elastic and versatile in their sexual behaviors.

There are animals on Earth who are very restricted in their sexual behaviors. Most species can only have sex during a brief time of the month or the year. Most animals are constrained to sex with members of the opposite sex within their own species. Most animals can only copulate in one position. Some animals are restricted to sex at one particular spot on Earth, with one particular member of the opposite sex of their own species, at one time of the year, or only once in a lifetime.

Humans are not like that.

Sex With a Ghost

A professor at a major university is giving a lecture on the super-natural. To get a feel for his audience, he asks, "How many people here believe in ghosts?"

About 90 students raise their hands.

"Well, that's a good start." he says. "How many of you have seen a ghost?"

About 40 students raise their hands.

"That's really good. Has anyone here ever talked to a ghost?"

About 15 students indicate they had.

"OK. Has anyone ever touched a ghost?"

Three students raise their hands.

"That's fantastic." He says. "Now let me ask one more question. Has anyone ever had sex with a ghost?"

Way in the back of the auditorium, Bubba raises his hand.

The professor takes off his glasses and says, "Son, in all the years that I have given this lecture, I have never met anyone who had sex with a ghost. Come down here and tell us about it."

The big redneck student replies with a nod and a grin, and walks down to the podium. The professor asks, "So tell us, what is it like to have sex with a ghost?"

Bubba replies, "Shucks, from way back there, I thought you said goats."

Humans are extremely diverse in their sexuality. They are capable of having sex in an overwhelming array of settings. They can have sex in any position, with the opposite sex, the same sex, different species, house pets, farm animals, houseplants, inanimate objects, and mechanical devices (and probably even with a ghost). They can have sex at any time of the month, any time of the year, and anywhere on Earth, in the sky, under water, or in outer space. Human genitalia are not at all particular. Humans are pansexual. A large proportion of humans have some capacity for so-called deviant sexual behaviors. Their individual preferences, at any given moment, are determined by their current libido levels, availability of partners, and a combination of genetic and cultural influences.

Diversity and Population Distributions

Populations of living things do not divide neatly into two categories. Rather, they fall into poorly demarcated groups, which often overlap. They are distributed in bell curves. For example, human skin color is not simply black or white. Skin color varies over a continuous range. More people fall in some areas of the range than in others, but there is somebody at every point on the range. Sexuality is that way, too. People are not just divided into male versus female, masculine versus feminine, or heterosexual versus homosexual. They vary continuously, with someone at every point on the range.

Sexual behavior is under the control of dozens, if not hundreds, of genes in the human genome. Each of these genes has multiple alleles, or variants, which are variable in potency. During adolescence and adulthood, a wide range of social experiences influence sexual preferences. Human cultures vary in degree of acceptance of non-heterosexual behaviors. When so many independent factors impact a person's sexuality, individual sexual behavior becomes stochastic. That is to say, it is randomized over a continuous range from extreme male behaviors to extreme female behaviors.

When traits are dependent on random input from multiple sources, each source is like the toss of a coin. Imagine you have two coins, and you toss them on the ground over and over, noting the number of heads and tails after each toss. Half of the times, the coins will land with one head and one tail up. One fourth of the times, they will both be tails, and one fourth of the times they will both be heads. The graph below represents this distribution.

Probability distribution for 2 coins

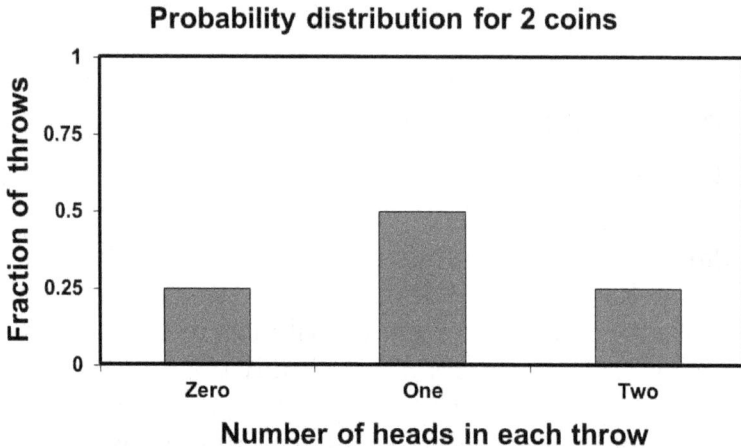

This result is exactly the same as the distribution of color in peas discovered by the monk Mendel in his famous experiments with the genetics of peas. When a plant grown from a yellow pea seed was cross pollinated with a plant grown from a green pea seed, one fourth of the resulting peas were green, one half were yellow-green, and one fourth were yellow.

Now, consider the same operation with six coins. The number of heads up will vary from zero to six with each toss, but, over time, the most common combination will be three heads and three tails. The next most common will be a two:four combination, followed by a one:five combination, etc. This is shown in the graph below. The row of bars starts to resemble a curve.

Probability distribution for 6 coins

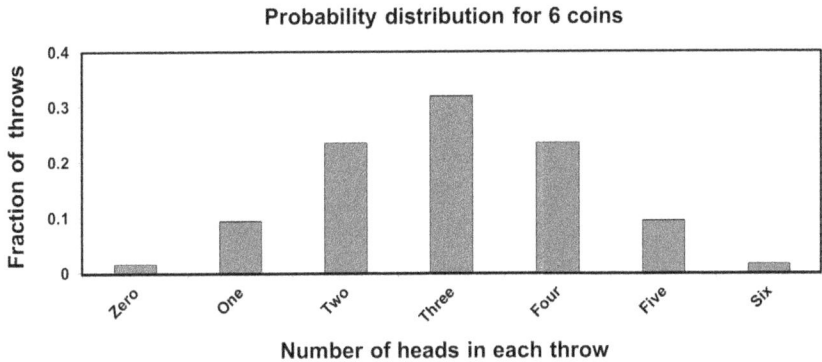

Next, instead of tossing the coins repeatedly, imagine that you have a thousand people, each holding six coins. Each of them will toss the six coins one time, and the number of heads up will represent some physical value. Think of the heads as genes that make people tall, and let the coin toss determine the person's height above five feet. When all the people have thrown their coins, you will have a population that is distributed by height, according to the following curve.

Height Distribution among 1000 people

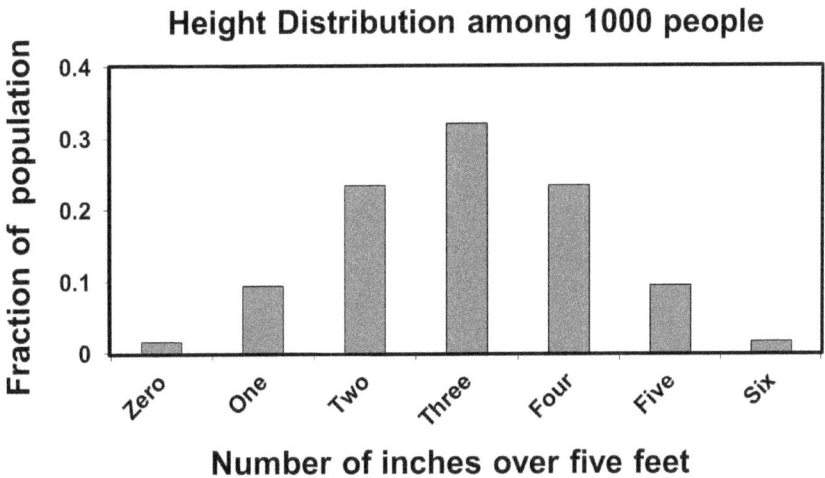

Of course, there are many more than six factors determining a person's height, and the distribution of height is much wider and smoother than shown in this curve. So, repeat the experiment with a larger number of coins, perhaps twenty. The likelihood of a person having all twenty coins land on heads, or on tails, becomes very low, but it can still happen. Most of the people will have their coin tosses distributed somewhere near the middle of the curve, with between six and fifteen coins landing heads up, as shown below.

Distribution for a large number of coins

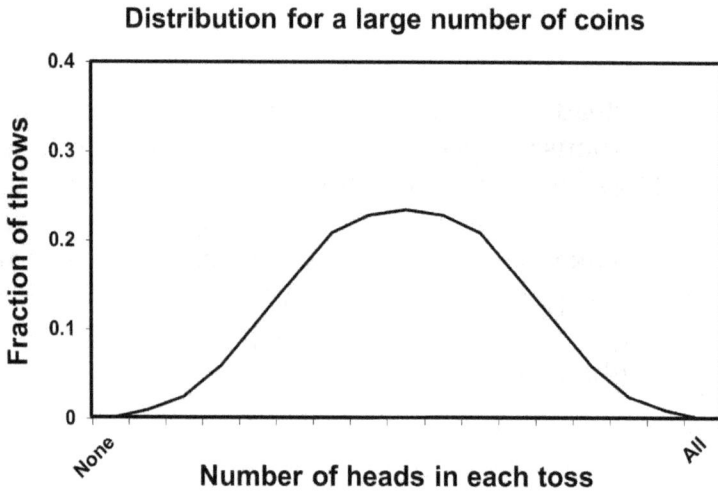

Number of heads in each toss

This is how biological populations are usually distributed. Characteristics that are determined by a large number of independent factors fall into bell-shaped curves, whether it is the length of antlers on male deer, the color of fur on grizzly bears, the number of stripes on zebras, or the height of American women. Height, though, is different from the other three characteristics. Humans have sexual dimorphism, which means that the males are a different shape and size than the females. Women are generally shorter than men, so their height curve would be skewed to one side of the scale, as shown below.

Height Distribution of Adult Women

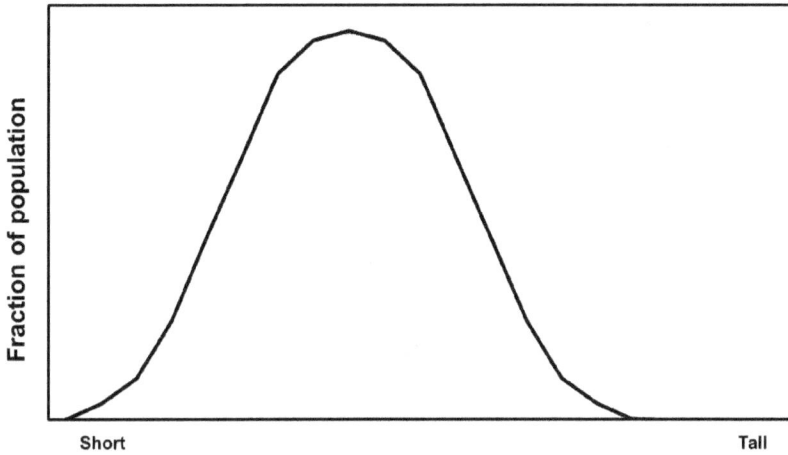

The height of men would be different from that of women. The men, on average, are taller, as shown below.

Height Distribution of Adult Men

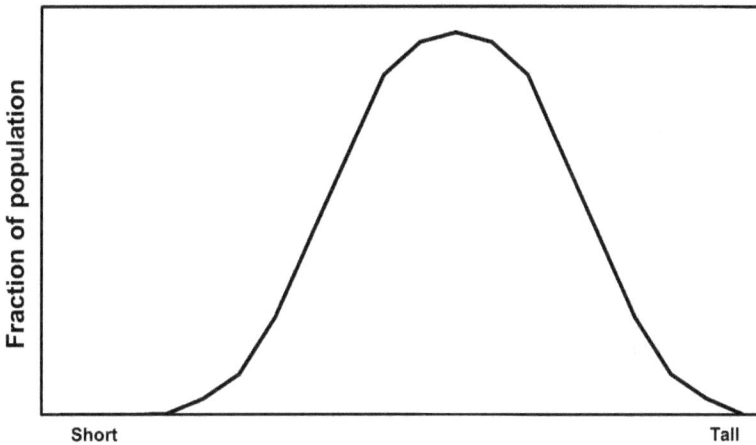

When the two curves are superimposed, a significant overlap is apparent. While men and women have different average heights, there are many women who are well over into the men's range and visa versa. This is called a bimodal population distribution. The population is divided into two groups or modes.

Height Distribution of All Adults

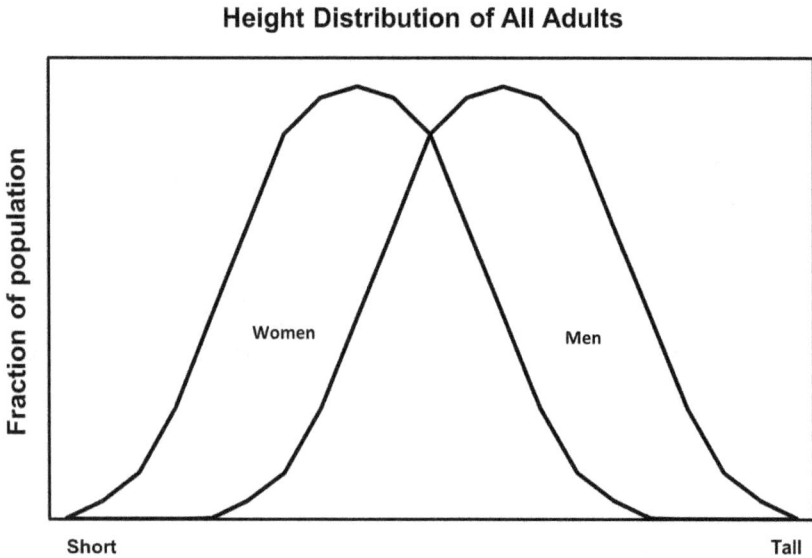

The same set of curves applies to many different parameters in biological systems. In this case, it demonstrates the difference in height between men and women. Males are, on average, taller than females. This same set of curves could also represent shoe size, amount of body hair, body muscle mass, voice pitch, and many other characteristics of the human population.

Sexuality is a cluster of characteristics that have bimodal distributions. They are not divided into discrete categories. Women tend to be more feminine and men tend to be more masculine, but there is significant overlap. Women tend to prefer sex with men, and men tend to prefer sex with women, but there is overlap. Women tend to fall in love with men, and men tend to fall in love with women, but there is overlap. There are some people in the middle, who are ambivalent, and there are some who cross over to the other side. The key to understanding human sexual diversity lies in understanding the manner in which randomness causes bimodal distributions of individual traits in a population.

Imagine a sexual-preference scale that ranges from heterosexual male behavior on one end to heterosexual female behavior on the other end. That is, the left end of the scale represents attraction to the female body, and the right end of the scale represents attraction to the male body. The distribution of sexual preference in the male population can be represented by a bell curve on the male side of the behavior range. Most males would fall on the right side of the scale.

Male Sexual Preferences

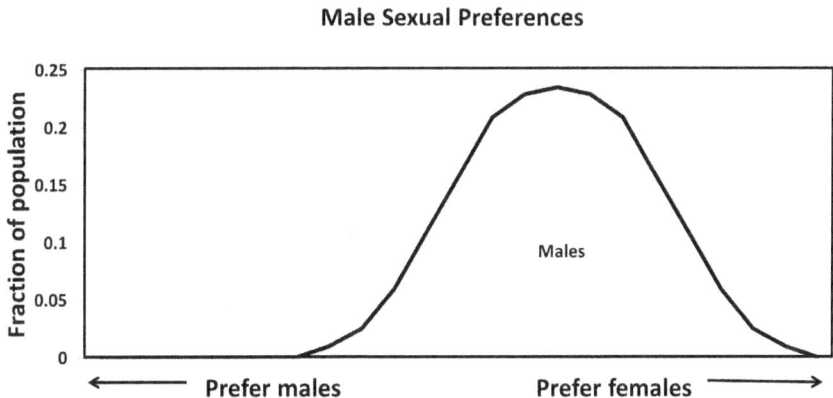

Female sexual preference can be represented by a bell curve in which most females fall on the female side of the behavior range.

Female Sexual Preferences

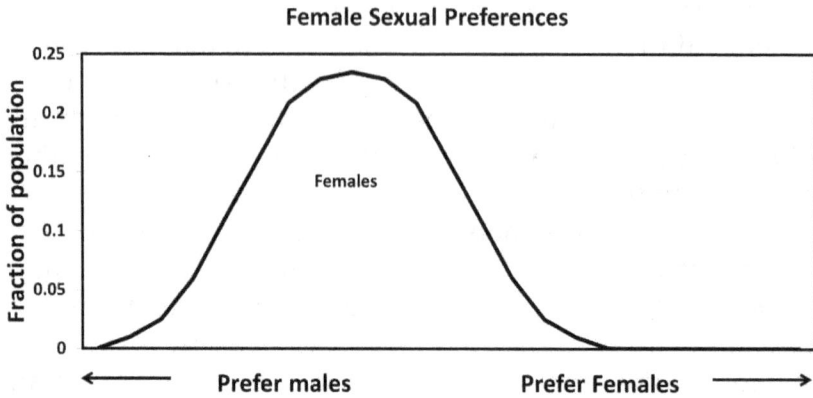

These two bell curves overlap in the middle, with some of the men falling by chance in the realm of female behavior, and some of the women falling in the realm of the male behavior. Those who fall in the overlap area are the individuals in the population with the ability to cross over in their sexual behavior.

Bimodal distribution of Sexual Preferences

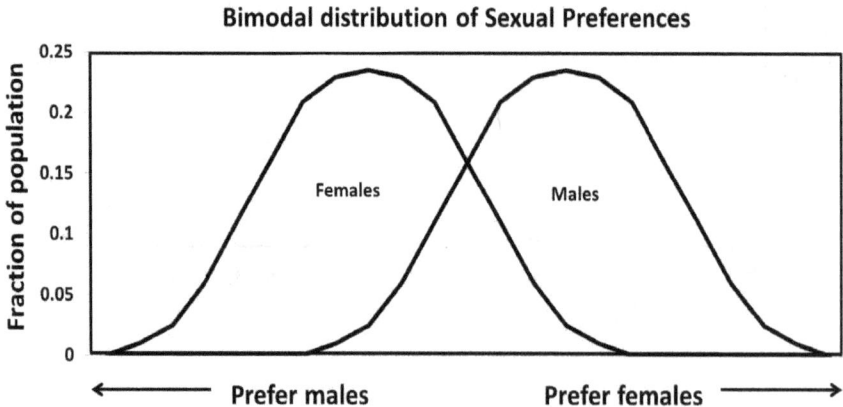

This means that for each sex, a small number of individuals will act strongly like the other sex in terms of their sexual preference. A larger number will have some ability to act like either sex, and the rest will only act like their own sex. These three groups are, respectively, the exclusive homosexuals, the bisexuals, and the exclusive heterosexuals. Within each sex, the majority will be exclusively heterosexual.

Diversity of Human Sexual Preferences

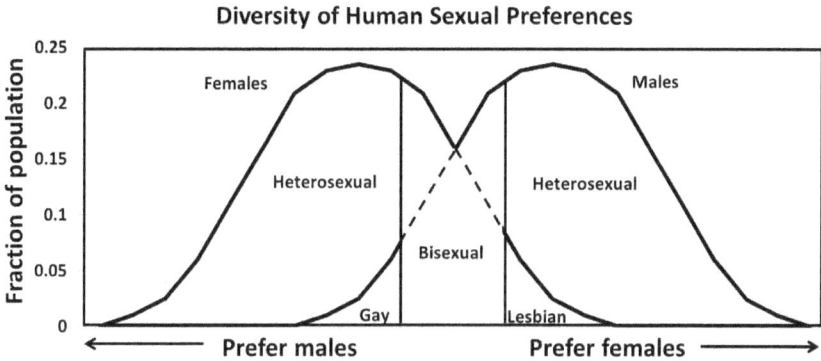

Many things impact the amount of crossover behavior that occurs in the overlap groups. Sometimes people are exposed to conditions where the opposite sex is unavailable. Some people live in cultures that condone or encourage homosexuality. Libido is variable, and increased libido causes people to be less selective about their partners. Under these conditions, members of a crossover population will use whatever partners are available. When released from constraints or compelled by loneliness, need, or lust, those people who are genetically able to do so will cross over to the behavior of the opposite sex.

This is why more homosexual behavior occurs in prisons or on naval ships at sea than in the general population. It is not because homosexuals are more prone to join navies or to commit crimes. It is simply because a large number of same-sex individuals are confined together, with no members of the opposite sex available. These conditions force individuals to choose between homosexual sex and no sex. There are many people in the overlap of the bell curves who would choose heterosexual sex over homosexual sex if given the option, but choose homosexuality over celibacy when forced to do so. Under compelling conditions, some people have the ability to behave as either heterosexuals or homosexuals.

Most people in the overlap group are bisexual. Most women who at some time in their lives have had sex with a woman have also had sex with a man. That is to say, bisexual women far outnumber exclusive lesbians. Likewise, most men who have had at least one sexual encounter with a man have also had sex with a woman. Bisexual men outnumber exclusively homosexual men.

This is one of the reasons that it is pointless to label people as heterosexual or homosexual, since they often change back and forth. Many homosexuals enter into heterosexual marriages and have families early in adulthood before they discover or admit to their sexual preferences. Many lesbians accept male lovers just for the purpose of fathering their children. Many bisexual women choose women for lovers because they feel that men are too aggressive and dangerous. Many other bisexual women lead exclusively heterosexual lives in order to conform to cultural norms. Many homosexual men marry women and have families. They either give up their homosexual lifestyles entirely, or keep extramarital male lovers. Many homosexual men have occasional opportunistic sex with women. Some homosexual men are married to women only for the length of a pair bond, and then resume their preferred lifestyles. Both men and women are known to alternate back and forth between sexes in their pair bonds. A woman will say that she has "given up on men for a while," or a man has "had it with women." When one type of relationship leaves a sour taste in the mouth, so to speak, some people are able to fall back on the other option.

Likewise, it is pointless to discuss whether homosexual behavior is simply a choice versus an inherited destiny. Obligate homosexuals, those on the extreme ends of the overlapped bell curves, do not have any choice in the matter. They simply do not have the ability to be heterosexual. And heterosexuals do not have any choice, because they simply do not have the ability to respond sexually to their own sex. They cannot engage in homosexual behavior. However, bisexuals do get to choose. For bisexuals, homosexuality is a choice, as is heterosexuality.

Gay Genes

The question inevitably arises whether people are born gay or born straight. Every person is born with a particular set point on the continuum from extreme male to extreme female sexual behavior. That is to say, there is a place on that continuum where a particular person is most comfortable. Where that place is for a particular person is probably controlled by many different genes and many different hormonal influences during development in the womb. For most of the population, that place is in one of the heterosexual areas, and the majority of the people can only respond sexually to the opposite sex. They are the obligate heterosexuals. A slightly smaller number of people are born to be in the overlapping portions of the bell curves, and can respond in some degree to either sex. They are the bisexuals. A smaller number are born to be in the extreme ends of the overlapping curves. These individuals do not have the capacity to respond sexually with the opposite sex. They can only respond to their own sex. They are the obligate homosexuals.

All people, though, can stray from their set points by some amount, according to their needs, their libidos, and their current situations. They can roam a certain distance from their set points when compelled, or simply allowed, to do so. Those who are born to be near the center of the scale can respond to either sex when the opportunity or need arises. Obligate heterosexuals and obligate homosexuals are too far from the middle range to be that flexible.

Bisexuals just have twice as many chances for a date on Saturday night.

Woody Allen

The proportion of the population that falls into these three groups is really not known with any accuracy. Alfred Kinsey estimated the bisexual portion to be about forty percent of the population. The number who actually exercise that option is not known.

The existence of a single gay gene, or even a small number of determinate genes, is unlikely. Sexual preference is not divided into two distinct categories like the two colors of Mendel's peas. Human sexual behavior is spread out over a smooth curve in the pattern typical of natural systems that are extremely multi-factorial and stochastic. That is to say, it appears to be a characteristic that has hundreds or thousands of contributing factors that sort independently and randomly.

The Other Components of Sexuality: Sex, Gender, Gender Preference, and Libido

Anatomic sex can be as indeterminate as sexual preference. People think of sex as a clear-cut matter of anatomy and genetics in which an individual is either male or female, but that is actually not correct. There are people who fall into an overlap area. Some males have a very small penis and appear to be females. Some females have a very large clitoris and look like males. Some babies are born with ambiguous genitalia, and cannot be classified anatomically. Rare individuals are born with both male and female genitals. Some people are anatomically female, but genetically male, because they have defective testosterone receptors. That is why genetic testing is required for some athletes.

Caster Semenya is a South African woman, born in the early 1990s. By age eighteen, she had become a world-class runner. Lean, muscular, and masculine in appearance, with a square jaw and a deep voice, she had small breasts, and had never had a menstrual period. When she began to win competitions on the international scene, her sex was questioned. Testing revealed that she has no ovaries or uterus. She has a small, shallow vagina, and two internal testes. She is, in fact, a male who is insensitive to the testosterone produced by her testicles, so she has the external genitalia of a female.

In 1843, a resident of Salisbury, Connecticut was challenged regarding voting rights because he was suspected of being a female and, therefore, not allowed to cast a ballot. Levi Suydam was required to undergo a medical exam, and was confirmed to have male genitalia. He was, however, also found to have a vagina, from which, he admitted, he had regular menstrual bleeding. He was able to engage in vaginal sex with men, and he admitted to having sexual interests in women, but whether he ever had sex with a woman is not known.

Anatomic sex in humans is distributed over a set of bimodal bell curves. There is a peak in the area of the average male genitalia and a peak in the area of the average female genitalia. But there are some individuals at every point along the entire range between the two peaks. The people in the valley between the two peaks must be identified by their genetics. Even this can be problematic, though. There are people who are not clearly genetically male or female. Sex in humans is determined by the sex chromosome, which comes in two variants, X and Y. The human male has one X chromosome and one Y chromosome (XY), while the female has two X chromosomes (XX). But other combinations are possible. Rarely, a child is born with two X chromosomes and a Y chromosome (XXY), or three X and one Y (XXXY), or even one X alone, or an X and a fragment of a Y. These people cannot be classified. The human race does not neatly separate into male and female categories.

Gender is different from sex. Gender is the sex of the persona that develops as personality emerges during childhood. It ranges from extremely masculine (think of Burt Reynolds) to extremely feminine (think of Marilyn Monroe). Some academics and scientists believe that the brain comes in male and female versions. Others think that gender is a learned characteristic. The truth is probably somewhere in between the two opinions. Gender is like any other inherited, loosely defined characteristic. Each of us is born with a range of possibilities, and where we end up in that range is determined by our environment.

Most males have a masculine gender, but to a variable degree. There are extremely masculine males, and mildly masculine males, and mildly feminine males, and very effeminate males. There is an occasional male who feels so strongly feminine that he insists he is a female in a male's body. Likewise, most females have feminine personas, but some display varying degrees of masculinity. There are females who are only comfortable in feminine attire, dripping with estrogen and makeup. There are those who are equally comfortable in pants or a skirt, in the shop or the kitchen, at work or in the nursery. There are a few who dress in men's clothing and urinate standing up.

George Sand was born Aurora Dupin in France in 1804. She left her husband after having two children and made a name for herself, figuratively and literally, as an authoress and a professional scandalous woman. She wore men's clothing whenever in public. She said they were more comfortable and less expensive than the elaborate women's costumes of the early nineteenth century in France. She smoked tobacco in public, preferring cigars. She publicly declared that she had no need for a husband, and she supported herself with her writing.

But George Sand was not a lesbian. She had a string of torrid affairs with powerful and influential men, including politicians, artists, poets, and musicians. Chopin was one of her better-known lovers, and she remained with him for years. She wrote profusely, and documented all her affairs. In all her letters and memoirs, there is only one hint of a romantic inclination toward a woman.

As with George Sand, things are not always as they seem at first glance. James was a patient who was brought to the ER in cardiac arrest with CPR in progress. He was fifty years old, obese, and in poor physical condition, suffering from diabetes and hypertension. Our resuscitation effort failed and he was declared "dead on arrival." During the resuscitation effort, all of his clothing was removed. An examination revealed bilateral mastectomy scars and female genitalia. James was a woman.

The mystery deepened when his wife and stepdaughter appeared in the ER. James had been married to this woman for twelve years and had helped raise her now sixteen-year-old daughter. Neither the wife nor the daughter had any clue that James was a female. The wife admitted that they had never engaged in sex, but she explained that her husband was impotent from his diabetes and hypertension. He had divulged this to her before they married, and they had never attempted sex. They had a Josephite marriage. The stepdaughter just knew James as her father. James was a woman who had felt so strongly about having a male gender that she managed to convince all those around her, even her own wife and step-daughter, that she was a man.

A transvestite prostitute named Pandora was a regular in our ER for years. S/he was riddled with an assortment of diseases accumulated through her incredibly unhealthy lifestyle. We treated him/her for rectal fissures, prostatitis, urinary tract infections, peri-rectal abscesses, and finally for the complications of HIV and AIDS. Pandora insisted that s/he was a woman, despite the presence of a penis and scrotum with testicles, and the absence of a vagina. S/he did have well developed breasts.

Pandora was once a loyal government worker in Washington, D.C. Under the name of Patrick, he worked out his career and retired after twenty years in the Social Security Administration. He had saved his money and looked forward to the day when he could get a sex-change operation. He went through all the psychiatric preparation and all the hormonal therapy to change his body and develop his breasts.

But Patrick was assaulted and severely beaten at a party one night and ended up in an ICU for months, with multiple complications of his injuries. He was eventually discharged, but had been rendered penniless. Worse yet, he had become a poor surgical candidate, due to the complications of his injuries. He could not undergo the surgical transformation from male to female. He lived out the rest of his life as Pandora, a tragic character stuck halfway between male and female. He had completely changed his gender, but was unable to change his sex.

Gender is how people feel about themselves. It is the ego component of sexuality, and it is separate from anatomic sex. Gender is the sexual identity that a person puts forward for the world to see, and it does not always match the person's sex.

A wonderful illustration of gender can be seen in the movie *Miss Congeniality*. The main character, Gracie Hart, played by Sandra Bullock, is an FBI agent who utterly lacks femininity. She fights like a man. She does not wear makeup. She does not even own a hairbrush. In the movie, she is assigned to go undercover at a beauty pageant, playing the role of a contestant. This requires that she transition from masculine to feminine gender, and the comparison of the two genders in the same person is as instructive as it is humorous. It is important to note that her sex, sexual preference, and gender preference do not change in the movie. Only her gender changes.

Gender preference is the gender to which a person is attracted. This is not the same as sexual preference. Just because a woman is turned on by sex with a man, that does not mean she wants a masculine person sharing her home. Most women like masculine men at least some of the time, but the degree is highly variable. Some women are put off by highly macho men, while other women find the macho personality a turn-on. Many women vary in their preference according to the time of the month. They find macho men fascinating during the two or three days near ovulation, and a bore the rest of the time.

My friend Chastity has a peculiar problem. She is a self-admitted lesbian and is in a long-term relationship with a woman. However, she confided that she has a male lover who she visits several times a year (really about once a month if possible). Chastity is in love with a woman, but she really prefers sex with men, especially during that time of the month when she has a strong desire for sex.

Gender preference in a woman depends, in part, on her hormone levels and mindset at the time. A woman in estrus, with a high estradiol level, will prefer more masculine, strong-jawed, broad-shouldered men. At other times of the month, she will prefer more gracile, delicate features on a male. A woman may prefer a less macho male for her steady, long-term partner, but she may also search out a stud when she is in heat.

There are women who have a strict preference for feminine features and behaviors in their partners. These are women who prefer effeminate males or females for their pair bond. Some women look for men smaller than themselves or want men who are docile and subordinate.

Likewise, most men prefer to bond with women who have feminine personalities. Most men like women who are domestic, take care of their appearances, and want to nurture children. But not all men share that preference.

I knew a young man named Michael who lamented to me one day that he had lost several girlfriends over the years to women, and he did not understand why. Michael has a gender preference for tomboys, that is, for women who have masculine personas. He encounters problems when he misidentifies lesbians as tomboys. Women who have a sexual preference for women are not necessarily masculine, but many lesbians do adopt masculine personas in order to advertise their sexual preferences. They are trying to attract other women, but sometimes they attract Michael instead.

Sexual preference indicates the anatomic sex to which the libido responds. Regardless of a person's genetic sex, gender, or gender preference, the libido may only respond to a male body or to a female body. A woman may prefer the company of a feminine personality, but that does not mean she can have sex with a female body. Likewise, she may be inclined to pair bond with a macho male, but that does not mean she prefers to have sex with him.

Chastity, who I mentioned about ten paragraphs back, is caught in this situation. She falls in love with women, but she is not very satisfied by sex with women. She prefers to have sex with men. That is because her libido responds better to the male anatomy, even though her emotions respond better to a feminine personality.

Remember the bimodal bell curve distributions. Most males engage in male mating behavior. Their libidos respond to female bodies. Likewise, most female libidos respond to male bodies. However, there is an overlap of the two populations, and it contains people who have libidos that can respond to both males and females to some degree. At the extreme tips of the crossover groups there are people who can only respond to their own sex.

Libido is a curious thing. Some people, a very few, simply have no interest in sex. None! At all! Other people, a very few, think about nothing else, and will take sex over food, family, law, and country. Nothing else matters! Most people fall in between. Libido is not at a fixed level for people. It changes constantly, depending on mood, health, age, and hormone levels. Libido is heavily influenced by psychiatric illness, fatigue, mood, environment, physical comfort, physical illness, drugs, alcohol, medications, and abstinence. Libido is notoriously fickle. It can be turned on by a glance, gesture, or phrase. But even at the height of passion, it can be turned off, shut down, by a single word or gesture. Libido is under the control of internal factors, and is also highly sensitive to external stimuli.

In a woman, libido follows a predictable cycle. It is low during menses, and rises to a plateau after menses. It abruptly rises and peaks about a day before ovulation, as the estradiol level rises. After ovulation, it recedes back to the pre-ovulation plateau. About a week before menses, it gradually falls.

Superimposed upon this baseline pattern, libido in a woman, or I should say in a feminine persona, responds to gifts, kind gestures, and other evidence of devotion. However, at times of high estradiol, it also responds to bravado and power. Libido is predictably increased by a safe environment and by caressing, touching, kissing, and other foreplay, as long as the caresses are welcome. It is turned off by any negative feelings, such as emotional trauma, jealousy, fear, and physical discomfort.

Males are more predictable than females, although they can also sometimes be enigmatic. The typical heterosexual male libido responds to any woman who shows an interest in him. It can be a smile, a gesture, or a few words. Like women, men respond to caresses, touching, kissing, and cuddling. Males also respond to static signals such as body shape and posture. This is why pornography has such a profound influence on males. They need nothing more than an hourglass outline in the 10:7:10 ratio to stimulate a response. Unlike females, who are selective about sex, males respond to all willing partners. A healthy young male is turned on by any female who enters his personal space and entices him.

In spite of that, human males are much more susceptible than females to internal influences. The male sexual response requires intact sympathetic and parasympathetic nervous systems and a healthy vascular system in order to achieve and maintain an erection. Unlike females, the human male cannot engage in the sex act unless he is sexually aroused.

Many illnesses affect his critical systems. Many medications -- especially psychiatric medications and blood pressure medications -- dampen the male sexual response, as does alcohol. Some illicit drugs, notably cocaine, ruin male libido. At one time, the British navy used a chemical, Potassium Nitrate, also known as saltpeter, to suppress libido in sailors at sea.

Male libido can also be felled by emotional signals. The male sexual response is notoriously fragile in the face of criticism from a sexual partner. The male ego is easily bruised by words or gestures. Once it is injured and the erectile response is lost, it can be difficult to recover.

In both males and females, libido changes with age. A man's libido is at its peak in the late teenage years and the early twenties, and gradually declines. An eighteen year old man can have sex several times an hour with the right partner. A fifty year old man, when properly inspired, can have sex several times a night, and an eighty year old, under the right conditions, might manage once a week. In women, libido typically increases with age, as they lose their fears and anxieties, and learn what their bodies need. They become aroused more easily as they age, up until menopause, and sometimes even after menopause.

Libido is important in the overall theater of sexuality because it determines how much a person wants to engage in sexual behavior. It is the factor that decides whether a marginally bisexual individual will crossover to engage in an opportunistic homosexual relationship when the need arises.

Unlike the other determinants of sexuality, the libido distribution curve is not bimodal. It does not divide into separate peaks for male and female, or masculine and feminine. The old belief that men have libido and women do not has been tossed into the trash bin of history. Both men and women are scattered all over the libido scale. Also, unlike the other distribution curves, libido is dynamic and not static. A person does not stay in one place on the range, but moves constantly. When libido changes, it affects the expression of all the other characteristics. That is the main reason that it is impossible to classify people as homosexual or heterosexual. As libido rises, people stray farther from their set points. People who have been only heterosexual start to stray over into the bisexual range, and engage in homosexual behaviors. People who were exclusively homosexual stray into the bisexual range and start to engage in heterosexual behaviors.

How the Pieces Make the Whole Person

Now that we have all these characteristics laid out on overlapping bell curves, let us step back and see how they combine. It is important to understand that these characteristics sort independently. That means they do not necessarily go together the way one would expect. This is so important a point that I am going to harp on it for a moment. There is no reason that anatomical sex, persona, gender preference, and sexual preference have to match. They do not come as matched sets. All combinations are possible, creating all kinds of unexpected diversity.

A few standard, well-recognized combinations encompass the majority of the population. Most men are masculine and prefer feminine women. And most women are feminine and prefer masculine men. These are referred to as *straight* people. Some masculine men prefer masculine women, that is, *tom-boys*. Michael is one of these men, and he often accidentally hits on lesbians. Masculine or feminine men who are sexually attracted to men are called *gay*. There are masculine women who prefer feminine women, the *butch-fem* combination. There are feminine women who prefer feminine women, and they are sometimes called *lipstick lesbians*. These are some of the named combinations. You can probably think of more examples. But these are only a few distinct hillocks on a broad, multi-dimensional landscape of human sexual behavior. Forget the rainbow. Human sexuality is a complex sculpture containing every conceivable combination of sex, gender, gender preference, and sexual preference. There are focal points that represent the more common combinations, the named groups, but between the focal points there is a great deal of landscape containing all possible variations and combinations.

The Rest of the Story

Homosexuality is the result of random distributions of sexual-preference determinants in the human population. But the presence of homosexuality is curious for another reason. There is a second half of the question. How do the genes for homosexuality stay in the gene pool? If homosexuals do not reproduce, then why does homosexuality persist in the human population, and how do the genes for homosexuality get perpetuated in the gene pool? The answer is that although obligate homosexuals do not reproduce, bisexuals reproduce very well. Because so many homosexuals have some degree of bisexuality, both gays and lesbians can be effective reproducers.

I will diverge for a moment and discuss a disease called Sickle Cell. This is a hereditary illness caused by a defective gene for hemoglobin. The normal gene is labeled Hemoglobin A, and the abnormal gene is Hemoglobin S. Every person has two copies of the Hemoglobin gene. Those with two A genes, denoted AA, are normal and healthy. Those with two S genes, denoted SS, are sickly, anemic, and in chronic pain. Without medical care, they die in childhood. Patients with one copy of each gene, AS, go through life anemic and have occasional pain, but survive with only minor disadvantages.

The Sickle Cell gene causes the body to make hemoglobin that crystallizes inside the red blood cells under low oxygen conditions. These crystals stretch the membranes of the red cells, and deform the cells into bizarre sickle shapes. The distorted, rigid, sickle cells create logjams in the capillaries. This slows or stops blood flow to the extremities and organs, causing severe pain and tissue death.

The Sickle Cell gene is prevalent among the black population that originated in Central Africa. This is curious. Why would a genetic abnormality persist in a population when it kills one forth of the offspring before they reach reproductive age? Why does the gene not die out? In order for a deleterious gene to persist in a population, it must offer some advantage that offsets the deleterious effects. In the case of Sickle Cell, the advantage involves susceptibility to malaria.

The malaria organism lives in the red blood cells, and is carried from one host to another in the blood ingested by mosquitoes. The hemoglobin crystals formed by Hemoglobin S kill the malaria organisms in the red cells. Patients with AS are immune to malaria. In Central Africa, malaria is so prevalent that only persons with AS can survive to adulthood. Most of the people with normal hemoglobin, those with AA, die from malaria in childhood, and all those with SS die from Sickle Cell disease in childhood, but most of those with AS survive to have children.

Of course *normal* and *abnormal* are relative terms. To a Central African native, the AS condition is normal, and the AA condition and the SS condition are abnormal disease states that kill people. Likewise, some cultures and social conditions consider homosexual behavior normal. It is better to think in terms of whether characteristics are adaptive or advantageous in certain circumstances than to label them as normal or abnormal. There are times and circumstances when homosexual behavior provides reproductive advantages. Ultimately, the reason that the Sickle Cell gene survives in the population is that, although persons with SS leave no offspring, the people with AS reproduce better than the people with AA.

This same principle applies to bisexuality. The genetics of sexual preference are much more complex than those of sickle disease. However, even though obligate homosexuals have low reproduction rates, homosexuality may persist in the population because bisexuals reproduce better than obligate heterosexuals.

Homosexuals and Reproduction

Remember that in humans both under primitive conditions, and in contemporary society, the primary function of sex is not to have babies. Sex is a social tool that is used to form alliances, cement relationships, heal rifts, and determine the pattern of sharing of resources. For humans, sex is much more a social device than a reproductive one. It occasionally results in conception, but is mostly used to construct a social environment in which to rear children.

A lesbian in today's Western culture can live with a long-term same-sex partner and choose from a variety of means to become pregnant. She can resort to artificial insemination, or submit to isolated acts of sexual intercourse with a male, or take up with a male in a heterosexual lifestyle until she becomes pregnant. Her lifestyle gives her a stable platform for raising a family, and a constant access to a sexual partner, without fear of unwanted pregnancy. She has complete control over when and by whom she becomes pregnant. When she does want to become pregnant, she can get access to a higher quality of genetic material than she could obtain if she were confined to men who are willing to commit to a long-term relationship. She needs only to select a willing male and convince him to have sex with her, a simple enough thing to do when she requires nothing from him except his gametes, which most males are anxious to give away. Of course, there may be social and legal complications.

The Genetics of Lesbian Motherhood

In modern Western culture, when a lesbian couple chooses to have a child, they generally use sperm from an unrelated, and often unknown, donor. This avoids legal complications related to the parental rights of the donor, but it means that the child is genetically related only to the natural mother. Under primitive conditions, this would not necessarily have been the case.

Primitive people were highly promiscuous. They lived in groups of fifty to one hundred related individuals. The women had sex with many men in the community for many different reasons. These women avoided having sex with closely related males such as their brothers and sons. However there was a high likelihood that a lesbian would be impregnated by a close relative of her partner. The child would then be genetically related to both female parents. A lesbian who is impregnated by her partner's brother bears a child who is the partner's niece or nephew. A lesbian impregnated by her partner's father, bears a child who is her partner's half-brother or half-sister.

Sharing of relatives for sexual services is taboo in modern culture, but occurred commonly in primitive cultures where siblings shared sexual favors with spouses. In some cultures a marriage consisted of a group of siblings from one family wed to a group of siblings from another family. Under such conditions, lesbians would have had the same opportunity as heterosexual women to become pregnant, and almost the same opportunity as heterosexual men to be genetic kin to their partner's offspring.

The male that the lesbian selects must, of course, be unencumbered by a relationship with another female. Even the most liberal-minded woman does not take kindly to her husband impregnating another woman. Fortunately, most lesbians are in close contact with a large community of men who are unencumbered by relationships with other women. Lesbians have the homosexual male population to choose from. These men may prefer to live with other men, but the majority of them are capable of having sex with a woman. Furthermore, they are generally cleaner, better groomed, more polite, better dancers, and more in tune with the feelings of women than are heterosexual men. A determined lesbian woman should have no difficulty finding a high-quality sperm donor.

Ellen was 51 when I knew her. She was a healthcare worker and a well-respected professional. She had never married. Early in her adulthood, she had wanted to have a child. She chose a man she liked and asked him to impregnate her. When I knew her, she had one grown son and three grandchildren. Ellen owned a large home, which she shared with several younger women with whom she was sexually active. She was also sexually active with men when the opportunity arose and the right man came along. Ellen illustrates again the reproductive potential of a not-entirely heterosexual person. It also reinforces that an individual may be an important, productive member of a community and still be on that part of the bell curve that crosses the centerline. Ellen is a true bisexual, equally comfortable with male and female sexual partners, although she prefers to live with women. She is also a very feminine person, and a talented belly dancer. For those readers who are curious, the man Ellen chose to father her child was married. She asked his wife first.

Meredith Baxter, the actress, is another example of a lesbian with high reproductive success. After three marriages to wealthy men, and after birthing five children, she publicly proclaimed that she is a lesbian. It would be more accurate to say that she has now adopted a lesbian lifestyle. She is, in fact, a bisexual, a person who is able to function well as a sexual partner to both men and women. Meredith has a feminine persona.

A co-worker of mine named Tina was exclusively heterosexual, until her marriage failed, leaving her with two children. She was consoled by, and eventually fell in love with, a female friend who had no children. Once the two of them settled into life together with the children, Tina's ex-husband re-entered the scene. The three adults remained on good terms for many years, co-parenting the children.

Meredith and Tina are good examples of people who are bisexual but live out a portion of their lives acting as if they are purely heterosexuals. This may, in fact, be where the majority of bisexuals reside. If bisexuals outnumber obligate homosexuals, then where are they? Why is their presence not evident in the population? There are several reasons. One is that bisexuals are not as visible as homosexuals. They lead conventional lives, for the most part, and can easily choose to lead a lifestyle that complies with social norms. That is to say, they can simply adopt the standard paradigm of heterosexuality and fade into suburbia with everyone else.

The other reason that bisexuals are not visible is that public opinion polarizes people into categories, either heterosexual or homosexual. Once a person is known to be in a homosexual relationship of any kind, he is often labeled publicly as homosexual, instead of being recognized as bisexual. Such is the case with several of the homosexuals presented in this text. Two of the bisexual women presented in this book complained to me that they have difficulty finding male lovers because they live with women in lesbian relationships. Men are confused by their enticements, and are hesitant to respond.

Bisexual women have a special advantage in childrearing, and this may be one of the main reasons that the behavior persists in the population. A bisexual woman who is left with children after an exhausted pair bond with a male can subsequently choose a female rather than another male for her next mate. It is a less-complicated relationship. There is no risk of further pregnancies. The children benefit from additional nurturing. A same-sex partner is not in reproductive competition with the ex-husband or the children. The mother has a mate to help support her children without being a danger to her children.

Tina and her ex-husband got along much better after she took up with a female lover. They may have felt more comfortable under those conditions than they would have if she were still alone, or if she had taken up with a male lover. Because her new partner is female, her ex-husband is not intruding on another male's territory when he comes to visit.

Like Tina, the great majority of lesbians who are raising children have retained the children from previous heterosexual relationships. By my own research, ninety-five percent of lesbian motherhood results from an earlier episode of a heterosexual lifestyle. When a woman with children divorces, and goes searching for a new mate for herself, she has an added burden of finding someone who will be tolerant of, and will not represent a danger to, her children.

A man has reproductive instincts that place him in competition with a woman's prior mate and his offspring. Even today, human males still occasionally reject, or even kill, the children of other males. The rate of childhood murder by stepfathers is ten times that of natural fathers. In my own twenty-five year experience, I have seen only two cases of children murdered by the natural fathers, but I have seen perhaps a dozen small children murdered by their mothers' boyfriends.

Homosexual males are less likely than lesbians to be raising children, but it does occur commonly. Usually one of the males has retained custody of children from a previous traditional relationship.

The 2000 U.S. census recorded approximately 600,000 same-sex couples, twenty-two to fifty-five years of age, in the United States. Two-thirds of these couples were male, and one-third were female. Of the total, thirty-nine percent were raising children below the age of eighteen. Males constituted forty percent of the childrearing couples and the females accounted for sixty percent. A quick calculation shows that twenty-four percent of male same-sex couples and seventy percent of female same-sex couples were raising children.

By comparison, sixty-eight percent of traditional heterosexual couples in the same age group were raising children. This means that lesbian couples have approximately the same parenting rate as heterosexual couples. This is an extremely enlightening calculation. Women embrace motherhood regardless of their sexual orientations!

There is a large difference in reproductive potential between male and female homosexuals. This is because females can engage in copulation in the absence of libido, and males cannot. Even today, self-declared lesbians have approximately the same fecundity as heterosexuals, and the great majority of those pregnancies are the result of heterosexual coitus. This was very likely true in the Stone Ages, too. Lesbianism was simply not much of an impediment to childrearing, because lesbians in a promiscuous setting had lots of reasons to have sex with men other than lust and desire, and they probably got pregnant as often as other women. They did not need artificial insemination.

Obligate homosexual males, however, probably did not have many offspring, because males cannot engage in copulation in the absence of desire. The penis does not become erect. Unlike lesbians, these obligate homosexual males were spared the burden of childrearing. They were the Sterile Caste. These were the people that had the free time to name patterns in the stars and observe where the sun rose each day. These were the priests who told the workers where to place the stones for Stonehenge, how to align the openings in the pyramids, and how to terrace the gardens at Machu Pichu. Ultimately, those cultures that utilized their Sterile Caste for the benefit of the population survived better than those that did not. That is why male homosexuality persists despite the absence of offspring among obligate male homosexuals.

While obligate male homosexuals do not reproduce, male bisexuals reproduce well. Under some conditions, they are more prolific than heterosexuals. A study of Toronto teenage pregnancy found that self-declared lesbian women were two and a half times more likely than straight women to have had a pregnancy in their teenage years. Even more surprising, self-declared gay men were four times more likely than straight men to have impregnated a woman during their teenage years.

Bisexual people start sexual activity earlier than heterosexuals, and become proficient at sex earlier in their lives. They have higher libido and are more inclined to engage in sex at higher frequencies than heterosexuals, simply because those persons with higher libido are able to stray farther from their set points and are more likely to be bisexual. They are more likely to become parents, and they become parents earlier in life than heterosexuals. They have more adaptability under duress. They are more adept at raising those children to adulthood under adverse conditions, because they have more options available to them than do heterosexuals. They have a wider range of potential partners to choose from. Bisexual women have access to higher-quality genetic material for their pregnancies, because they are not constrained to men who are willing to commit time and resources to them. Bisexual men have more casual access to women, and are more available when women are in estrus and want an attractive casual contact.

Homophobia

I suspect that the reproductive potential of homosexual males may be the main reason, from an evolutionary point of view, that heterosexual males ostracize homosexual males. To understand why, it is necessary to diverge and discuss a type of insect, a dung beetle. These are in the same family as the rhinoceros beetles. Rhinoceros beetles display sexual dimorphism. The males of this family are much larger than the females, and have large anterior horns, which they use when they fight over females and territories. Specifically, male dung beetles fight over piles of dung that attract large numbers of females. The male who is in control of a pile of dung gets to mate with the females it attracts. He will fight off any other male that approaches.

Some males in the species are smaller and do not have horns. These males slip past the horned males, un-noticed, because they look and act like females. This reproductive strategy is called gender mimicry. They can then browse among the females, waiting for the horned male to be distracted, either mating with a female or involved in a fight with another male. They take that opportunity to mate with the females. This is called *sneaking behavior* in beetles, but in humans it would be called cuckolding.

Among humans, effeminate homosexual and bisexual males integrate better with females than do heterosexual males. They have more feminine behavior and personalities. They are more sensitive to the emotional needs of females. They have more common interests with females. Their thought processes and social skills are more attuned to female social settings. They are non-threatening. They fit in well with females, and they will be close at hand when a female nears ovulation and seeks an opportunistic lover.

Effeminate behavior in males is a type of gender mimicry. It allows bisexual men to have access to women through a different pathway than that used by masculine males. I suspect that this ability of effeminate males to cuckold is why heterosexual males have an instinctive distrust of effeminate males and try to drive them away. Human males with effeminate behaviors are not declining the opportunity to reproduce. Rather, they are using an alternate reproductive strategy. The macho heterosexual males are confused and frustrated by effeminate males who seem to be better liked by females for traits that the macho males cannot emulate.

Interestingly, this may be why homosexual males are ostracized, while homosexual females are not. Homosexual males are threatening to heterosexual males because they can sneak in and impregnate females who "belong" to the heterosexual males. Lesbians are not threatening to anyone. They do not take mates or resources from heterosexual women. They cannot cuckold heterosexual men. They only occasionally take a mate from a heterosexual man, but the man rarely makes a fuss about it because of the stigma of losing a mate to a member of the opposite sex. At most, lesbians are considered a curiosity. Heterosexual men find them intriguing because the idea of two women being aroused at the same time is twice as interesting as one aroused woman. Heterosexual women are basically neutral to lesbians.

Some conflict does occur between lesbians and other groups. When a lonely man approaches a lesbian and is rejected arbitrarily, he may become angry. Also, there is some ostracism of bisexual women by exclusively lesbian women. There are several possible explanations for this, but it is probably similar to the ostracism of homosexual males by heterosexual males. The lesbians know how to compete against other women in their relationships, but they are confused when they have to compete against men. A lesbian woman who dates a bisexual woman finds herself facing male competitors who she cannot fully emulate.

The ostracism of Western, especially American, male homosexuals causes men to be placed into polarized categories of either heterosexual or homosexual. Adversity between the two groups tends to create an "us versus them" mentality in which heterosexual men shun all men who show any evidence of homosexual behavior. Heterosexual males are afraid of being misidentified by their peers as homosexual. As a result, most straight men refrain from any behaviors that might create any stigma of homosexuality. They don't hug, kiss, hold hands, engage in social grooming, or speak to each other in public bathrooms. They avoid any possibility of being mis-identified as homosexual. They avoid any display

Boolean Logic and Homosexuality

Here is an exercise in Boolean logic applied to human sexuality. Let the female population be divided into sets as follows: (Identical sets can be constructed for males.)

Women who can fall into romantic love with women
Women who cannot fall into romantic love with women

Women who can be sexually aroused by women
Women who cannot be not sexually aroused by women

Women who have had sex with women
Women who have not had sex with women

Women who can fall into romantic love with men
Women who cannot fall into romantic love with men

Women who can be sexually aroused by men
Women who cannot be not sexually aroused by men

Women who have had sex with men
Women who have not had sex with men

Here are six pairs of mutually exclusive categories, which combine to create $2^6 = 64$ different groups of women. Women in any of the following groups might self-declare to be lesbians:

Any woman who can fall in love with another woman (32 groups):
Of the remaining 32, any woman who can be sexually aroused by women (16):
Of the remaining 16, any woman who has had sex with a woman, but not a man (4):

218 Why Do Fools...?

and finally, of the remaining 12, any woman who is not sexually aroused by men (6).
Incredibly, women in 58 of these 64 groups could self-declare to be lesbians.

Some lesbian women are prejudiced, defining lesbians as only those persons who can fall in love with and be aroused by women, but cannot fall in love with or be aroused by men. This definition requires a woman to meet four out of 6 categories. Because each category that must be met reduces the number of groups by one half, this reduces the number of groups meeting that definition of lesbianism to only 4 of the 58 groups. The other 54 self-declared groups are ostracized for not being "true" lesbians.

This exercise illustrates why it is so difficult to count the number of homosexuals in the population. There is no clear definition of homosexuality. Statistics on homosexuals are based upon self-declared homosexuals. Women, and men, refer to themselves as homosexual for many different reasons.

of affection with other men because they fear being ostracized themselves. Oddly, the underlying reason that heterosexual men ostracize effeminate men is because they are jealous of the closer relationship that the effeminate men have with women.

Heterosexual women, on the other hand, do not ostracize lesbians, so women have no reason to fear being misidentified as homosexuals. Therefore, women are comfortable engaging in all sorts of personal contact, mutual grooming, and casual affection in public.

...that they are endowed by their Creator with certain unalienable Rights, that among these are Life, Liberty and the Pursuit of Happiness.

Thomas Jefferson

Disapproval of homosexuality cannot justify invading the houses, hearts, and minds of citizens who choose to live their lives differently.

Harry A. Blackmun,
U.S. Supreme Court Justice

14

Sexual Preference in the Animal World

Human homosexual practices have been labeled variously as "perverted," "un-natural," and "alternative," relegating them to the general class of "other than normal" behaviors. However, homosexuality is surprisingly widespread in nature, and so are a large variety of other non-heterosexual reproductive strategies. We think of the sexual world as being divided into male and female, but there are at least five discreet sexes among animals, plus a variety of asexual reproductive patterns, and some patterns that fall in between sexual and asexual. Some scientists and doctors count five different sexes among humans, and others think that anatomical sexuality in humans covers a gradual transition from male to female.

Outside the world of primates, there is great variation in sexuality. Among animals, there are species that are divided into male and female for a lifetime, like mammals. There are other species in which the young adults are all male, and as they increase in age they turn into females. This includes many fish. But there are many other fish that can change back and forth between male and female according to population demand. There are species that are true hermaphrodites, in which each individual has both male and female sex organs. All the earthworms are in this group. There are species in which there is only one sex, which is called female by default. Rotifers, some reptiles, and some birds are in this group. Clearly, what is "natural" in terms of sex is highly diverse.

Certain species of lizards, notably the whiptail lizards, have only females, and they manage to reproduce successfully. They still mate, though, and have a rudimentary form of copulation. Two females court, and then take turns mounting each other in the fashion of heterosexual lizards. Although there is no transfer of genetic material between the two females, the mounting is still necessary. A female whiptail lizard will not produce eggs unless she has been mounted by another female.

In 1998, two male chinstrap penguins in the Central Park Zoo in Manhattan formed a pair bond that lasted for years. During successive mating seasons they engaged in the typical displays of physical affection that identify a bonded pair. They remained bonded, year after year, despite the availability of female penguins. One year, being without an egg, they attempted to incubate a rock. By coincidence, a female penguin had abandoned an egg, leaving it orphaned. The enterprising zoo staff gave it to the same-sex male pair, who proceeded to successfully raise the female chick to adulthood. The ultimate sexual orientation of the chick has not been published. Homosexuality is common among penguin species, and same-sex pair-bonding has been documented among 130 other species of birds.

Most mammal species that utilize polygamy as a reproductive strategy have several other characteristics in common. First, they are sexually dimorphic, with the males being larger than the females. Second, the males mature later in life than the females. And third, some of the males are not interested in mating with females, but attempt to mate with other males. This is true among sheep, elk, gorillas, bonobos, and humans, to name a few examples.

Among our closest primate kin, the bonobos, homosexual behavior is rampant. All bonobo adults are bisexual. Same-sex relations are almost as frequent as heterosexual relations. Females have sex with other females, usually in the missionary position. They also engage in oral sex. Males have sex with other males in several positions and also engage in a curious behavior called "penis fencing," the specific details of which will be left to the reader's imagination.

Finally, homosexual behavior has been present in human societies since the Stone Age. References to same-sex liaisons are found as far back as the earliest archeological records. In Stone Age cultures that buried men and women differently, archeologists have found transsexual graves in which a member of one sex is buried in the position of the other sex, and with grave goods typically found with the other sex. The behaviors of prehistoric humans are still observable, represented in the few Stone Age cultures that remain in existence in the isolated places on Earth. Ford and Beach, in their landmark text, *Patterns of Sexual Behavior*, reported that homosexuality was accepted by forty-nine of seventy-six primitive cultures studied, including eighteen American Indian tribes. Homosexuality is simply a part of the natural spectrum of human sexual behaviors. Like all the other primitive instincts in the human repertoire, it continues to exist because it is a viable reproductive strategy.

15

The standard dogma

Most of the people I have known over the years were simply heterosexual. They took the straight path and adhered to the standard dogma. The women looked for men who could support them and protect them. The men looked for women who could birth and raise their children. Both men and women looked for both long-term relationships and short-term relationships. Most of the time, they did not know what they were looking for until they found it.

With rare exceptions, the men have been the primary providers for the couples I have met. Many of the women worked, but they usually earned less than their husbands. The men most often complained that they were not getting enough affection, that is, sex, from their wives, or that their wives were spending too much money. The women most often complained that their husbands wanted too much sex, or created too much mess, or did not provide enough money.

Most of the people I have met still believe in monogamy, although many of them suspect that something is not quite right with the idea. They hedge their bets with terms like serial monogamy. I think many of them suspect that the traditional

dogma is seriously flawed. Their suspicions reflect dissatis-
faction with their post-romantic relationships. Certainly, most
of them are unhappy to some degree, and they do not know
why. Usually, they blame their spouses or themselves. I have
never heard any of them talk about pair-bonding, though.
The linkage of pair bonds to humans is a new meme, one that
has the potential to alleviate the shame, guilt, and resentment
that accumulates in long-term relationships.

Most people try to find long-term mates, and most of
them eventually succeed. They do so with only a rudimentary
understanding of the mechanisms involved in mate selection.
They play their roles, follow their scripts, and make their decisions with no awareness of the impact their actions have upon
world politics or the course of human history.

For the most part, humans operate on their instincts and do
not know why they do what they do. They just do what feels
right. This was the case with my junior colleague Caroline.
We have come around full circle and we can now answer the
question that I originally asked of her. Why would she allow
men to overrule the instructions written within her genetic
program? The question must be broken into fragments, which
can be answered individually. The easiest and most superficial answer is that her parents and religious leaders taught her
to do so. They spent a great deal of effort teaching her that she
should have only one sexual partner in her life, and that she
should stay with him her entire life. That is why the behavior
occurred in her as an individual. But it does not explain why
she would feel compelled to continue the behavior.

What have women obtained from this behavior called
monogamy that reinforces the behavior? Until a few decades
ago, Caroline would have been compelled to stay with her
husband because she would have had no good alternative.
There would have been no other way for her to adequately
provide for herself and her child except by attaching herself
to a man and living off his earnings in exchange for her moth-
ering of his children. What women obtained from monogamy
was financial security. Caroline, though, is highly skilled and

employable and she lives in a society that allows her to support herself. She is able to leave her husband, and she did.

Other parts of the question deal with her culture. How did monogamy originate in human cultures in the first place? Monogamy is a human invention. It was developed about five thousand years ago to accommodate the needs of patriarchal societies attempting to control property inheritance through control of paternity. But what advantage does monogamy provide that causes it to be retained in human cultures, and why is it the only family structure endorsed by Caroline's culture and religion? Monogamy persists because it provided the most stable family platform for rearing and educating children. Historically, it stabilized cultures by facilitating the handing down of memes from one generation to the next. It aided the accumulation of a body of cultural knowledge, which eventually developed into a body of technical knowledge. Those religions and nations that could keep the parents of children together long past their pair bond eventually became more technologically advanced than promiscuous societies. They were able to invest more in their children, and to better educate their children. In the incessant competition between cultures, the monogamous ones surpassed the others economically, politically, and militarily. Caroline is a member of a monogamous culture.

Caroline frets about leaving her husband because she is fearful of the effect of divorce on her child. She is aware that in our modern society, children do best in a two-parent home. They perform better in school, have fewer behavioral problems, and are more likely to go to college.

None of that makes it any easier, though, for Caroline to stay in a post-romantic relationship, and all romantic relationships eventually do become post-romantic. All couples, whether homosexual, bisexual, or heterosexual, fall in love and form pair bonds. After a few years, their pair bonds dissipate, their ego boundaries come back, and they are caught off guard by this unexpected turn of events. Some couples struggle through, and eventually transition to a viable post-romantic relationship, with varying degrees of emotional trauma. Others give up, and resign themselves to failure, never understanding the problems they face. They leave one relationship and are doomed to enter another with the same outcome.

When a relationship between two people fails, the fault lies not in their morals or their resolve, but in their failure to realize that the pair bond is a term-limited process, and that a transition to a different kind of relationship will have to occur after a few years. A better understanding of basic human nature and individual human needs will alleviate the discomfort of that transition. It will either improve couples' chances of a successful transition to a post-*romantic* relationship, or reduce the emotional trauma of transition to a post-*marital* relationship.

Of course, the life-long, post-romantic relationship may not be ideal for everyone, especially now that so many people remain childless. Remember the adaptive function of a post-romantic relationship. It facilitates the rearing of children through college. Childless couples do not have this social obligation, and should be allowed to opt out of marriages without shame, guilt, or resentment. They have no obligation to each other beyond common courtesy. Like Dan and Alicia, they are free to go their separate ways. This also applies to most homosexual couples, and is one of the reasons that homosexual relationships are generally not as enduring as the standard heterosexual couples. There are no shared offspring. By extension, couples who have raised their children should recognize that they have done their service to their offspring and their society. Like my friend Katlyn, couples with grown children should rejoice in the successful outcome of their marriage, cast off the social mandate of monogamy, and embrace their abilities to fall in love again with whomever they choose.

16

Conclusion

The initial question posed in the introduction to this book was, "If humans were meant to live together as lifelong couples, then why is it so hard to do?" The answer is that humans are *not* meant to live together as lifelong couples. Humans are not a monogamous species. They are a pair-bonding species. People choose to try to live together as lifelong couples because it provides a solution to a problem that is thrust upon them by their technological success. Humans have become so adept at tool use and symbol manipulation that the time required to learn all the basic skills of society now far exceeds the duration of the natural human pair bond.

Modern, highly technological cultures function better when humans choose to live monogamous lifestyles, and so the governments and religions that have survived are those that have encouraged monogamy and discouraged promiscuity. Monogamy is *generally* the best system for rearing children in our complex culture. It strengthens a society. But it necessitates that men and women live together as couples for a much longer time period than is natural or comfortable. When their discomfort grows so great that the family becomes dysfunctional, then monogamy may not be the best model for either the children or society.

Most of the misery that accompanies failed relationships arises from unrealistic expectations. Young lovers are disillusioned when their pair bonds gradually expire. As their ego-boundaries return, they start to express themselves as individuals again. In doing so, they begin to accumulate the guilt, shame, and resentment that prevents them from transitioning to a healthy, resilient, post-romantic relationship. This can be prevented if couples are educated regarding the true nature of romantic love. Those who are aware that humans are not naturally monogamous, but form time-limited pairs, will expect and prepare for a smooth transition in their relationships.

Some pair bonds, even those that are irresistibly strong at first, are simply not destined to transition into stable post-romantic relationships. When the pair bond expires, couples may discover unpleasant things about themselves and their partners. They may find that they have incompatible social networks. One of them may change sexual preferences, or change life goals. Sometimes they just find that they can't stand one another, and that they have "irreconcilable differences." It is essential that couples recognize that these are natural outcomes when marriage choices are based on pair bonds. People learn a lot about each other in four to seven years. When this occurs, they should recognize that they got into this together, and they should help each other get out emotionally intact. They should continue to treat each other with the courtesy and respect due to life-partners, as they transition from a post-romantic relationship into a post-marital relationship.

A stable, functional post-romantic relationship is the best environment for raising children, but a stable, functional post-marital relationship runs a close second best. There are other good options as well: same-sex couples jointly raising their combined families, dioecious households, and matrilineal households. Ultimately, any family setting that provides a safe, loving environment, adequate financial support, consistent discipline, and wholesome values will produce healthy children.

In the final analysis, children are what it is all about. Propagation is the goal of life. Some of us will propagate ourselves, and some of us will propagate our ideas. Our purpose is to carry genetic and/or cultural information forward in time to the next generation through the mixing of gametes and the nurturing of children. Ultimately I must agree with Somerset Maugham. Falling in love is a trick played on us by nature in order to perpetuate the species. That is why fools fall in love.

References

Adams, C. (2007, October 19). Who's your daddy? Is it true 10–15 % of children in modern society were not sired by their putative fathers? *The Straight Dope*. Retrieved from http://www.straightdope.com

Adovasio, J. M., Page, J., & Soffer, O. (2007). *The invisible sex: Uncovering the true roles of women in prehistory*. New York, NY: HarperCollins Publishers.

Ahrons, C. R. (1994). *The good divorce*. New York, NY: HarperCollins Publishers.

Ames, A., Burke, D., & Ellis, L. (1987, December). Sexual Orientation as a continuous variable: A comparison between the sexes. *Archives of Sexual Behavior, 16* (6), 523–529. Doi: 10.1007/BF01541716

Anderson, K. G. (2006). How well does paternity confidence match actual paternity? Evidence from worldwide paternity rates. *Current Anthropology 47* (3), 513–521.

Armstrong, K. (1994). *A History of God: The 4,000-year quest of Judaism, Christianity and Islam*. New York, NY: Ballantine Books.

An arrangement of marriages. (1993, January 1). *Psychology Today*. Retrieved from http://www.psychologytoday.com

Aubuchon, V. (2010). *World population growth history*. Retrieved from Vaughn's Summaries website: http://www.vaughns-1-pagers.com

Ayres, B. D. (1991, November 21). Fertility doctor accused of fraud. *The New York Times*. Retrieved from http://www. nytimes.com

Badgett, M. L., & Sears, B. (2004). *Same-sex couples and same-sex couples raising children in California: Data from Census 2000*. Retrieved from eScholarship Repository, University of California: http://repositories.cdlib.org/uclalaw/ williams/census/california.2000

Bailey, J. M., Keller, M. C., Macgregor, S., Martin, N. G., Morley, K. I., Shekar, S. N., ... & Zietsch, B. P. (2008, July 1). Genetic factors predisposing to homosexuality may increase mating success in heterosexuals. *Evolution and Human Behavior, 29*, 424–433. Doi: 10.1016/j.evolhumbehav.2008.07.002

Baker, J. A., Fox, C. A., & Wolf, H. S. (1970). Measurement of intra-vaginal and intra-uterine pressures during human coitus by radio-telemetry. *Journal of the Society for Reproduction and Fertility, 22*, 243–251.

Baker, R. (1996). *Sperm wars*. New York, NY: Perseus Books Group.

Bancroft, J. (2005). The endocrinology of sexual arousal. *Journal of Endocrinology, 186*, 411–427. doi: 10.1677/joe.1.06233

Barash, D. P. (n.d.). *Deflating the myth of monogamy*. Retrieved from Trinity University website: http://www.trinity. edu/rnadeau/fys/barash%20on%20monogamy.htm

Batt, J., Hall, S., Hendricks, C., & Olson, D. (1998). *Gender differences in physical attraction*. Retrieved from Miami University, Oxford, Ohio website: http://www.units. muohio.edu/psybersite/attraction/gender.shtml

Battles, M. (2004). *Library*. New York, NY: W. W. Norton and Company, Inc.

Baumeister, R. F., & Vohs, K. D. (2004). Sexual economics: Sex as female resource for social exchange in heterosexual interactions. *Personality and Social Psychology Review, 8* (4), 339–363.

Beach, F. A., & Ford, C. S. (1951). *Patterns of sexual behavior.* New York, NY: Harper and Row.

Beil, D., Deininger, H., Kunz, G., Leyendecker, G., & Wildt, L. (1996). The dynamics of rapid sperm transport through the female genital tract: Evidence from vaginal sonography of uterine peristalsis and hysterosalpingoscintigraphy. *Human Reproduction, 11* (3), 627–632.

Ben-Zeev, A. (2008, September 12). When do we fall in love? [Web log message]. Retrieved from Psychology Today website: http://www.psychologytoday.com/blog/in-the-name-love/ 200809/when-do-we-fall-in-love

Besl, J. (n.d.). Births to unmarried moms increase sharply [Web log message]. Retrieved from The Community Research Collaborative Blog website: http://crcblog.typepad.com/crcblog/births-to-unmarried-moms-increase-sharply.html

Blomberg, S. P., Kaplan, G., MacFarlane, G. R., & Rogers, L. J. (2007). Same-sex sexual behavior in birds: Expression is related to social mating system and state of development at hatching. *Behavioral Ecology, 18,* 21–33. Doi 10.1093/beheco/arl065

Blumberg, S. L., Markman, H. J., & Stanley, S. M. (2001). *Fighting for your marriage.* San Francisco, CA: John Wiley and Sons, Inc.

Boswell, J. (1995). *Same sex unions in pre-modern Europe.* New York, NY: Random House.

Brooke, J. (2011, March 17). Did feminism cause divorce? *Huffington Post.* Retrieved from http://www.huffington-post.com

Brooks, M., Chiafari, F. A., Houtz, T., & Wenk, R. E. (1992). How frequent is heteropaternal superfecundation? *Acta Genet Med Gemellol (Roma), 41* (1), 43–47. Retrieved from http://www.ncbi.nlm.nih.gov/pubmed/1488855

Brown, A. (n.d.). *George Sand: An amazing woman*. Retrieved from http://www.amybrown.net/women/george.html

Browne, J. (2006). *Dating for Dummies* (2nd ed.). Hoboken, NJ: John Wiley and Sons.

Browning, D. (1989, October 11). Rethinking homosexuality. *The Christian Century*, 911–916. Retrieved from http://www.religion-online.org

Buss, D. M. (1985, January/February). Human mate selection. *American Scientist, 73*, 47–51.

Buss, D. M. (1989). Sex differences in human mate preferences: Evolutionary hypotheses tested in 37 cultures. *Behavioral and Brain Sciences, 12*, 1–49.

Buss, D. M. (2003). *The evolution of desire*. New York, NY: Perseus Books Group.

Buss, D. M., & Meston, C. M. (2007). *Why humans have sex*. Available from Archives of Sexual Behavior. (UMI no. 36: 477–507). Doi 10.1007/s10508-007-9175-2

Buss, D. M., & Schmitt, D. P. (1993). Sexual strategies theory: An evolutionary perspective on human mating. *Psychological Review 100* (2), 204–232.

Cacioppo, J. T., & Patrick, W. (2009). *Loneliness: Human nature and the need for social connection*. New York, NY: W. W. Norton & Company.

Caldwell, J. C., & Caldwell, P. (1990, May). High fertility in Sub-Saharan Africa. *Scientific American, 262* (5), 118–125.

Canfora, L. (1990). *The vanished library: A wonder of the ancient world*. Berkeley: University of California Press.

Cecil Jacobson. January 10, 2012. Retrieved January 15, 2012, from Wikipedia website: http://en.wikipedia.org/wiki/Cecil_Jacobson

Cecil B. Jacobson [encyclopedia article]. (n.d.). Retrieved from NationMaster website: http://www.nationmaster.com/encyclopedia/Cecil-Jacobson

Census reports more than 130,000 same-sex couples say they're married. (2011, September 28). *Associated Press.* Retrieved from http://www.foxnews.com

Center for Gender Sanity. (2001, August 16). *Diagram of sex and gender.* Retrieved from http://gendersanity.com/diagram.shtml

Chandra, A., Copen, C., Mosher, W. D., & Sionean, C. (2011). Sexual behavior, sexual attraction, and sexual identity in the United States: Data from the 2006–2008 National Survey of Family Growth. *National Health Statistics Reports; no 36.* Hyattsville, MD: National Center for Health Statistics.

Childfree. (2010, July 20). Retrieved July 21, 2010, from Wikipedia website: http://en.wikipedia.org/wiki/Childfree

Circumcision Information and Research Pages. (2008, August 9). *Foreskin sexual function/circumcision sexual dysfunction.* Retrieved from http://www.cirp.org/library/sex_function/

Code of Hammurabi. (L. W. King, trans.). Retrieved from Internet Ancient History Sourcebook website: http://www.fordham.edu/halsall/ancient/hamcode.asp#horne

Cohen, K. M., & Savin-Williams, R. C. (2010, November 16). Can men have sex with men and still call themselves straight? *The Good Men Project.* Retrieved from AlterNet website: http://www.alternet.org/story/148876/

Cohn, D. (2011). *Census Bureau: Flaws in same-sex couple data.* Retrieved from Pew Social and Demographic Trends website: http://www.pewsocialtrends.org/2011/09/27/census-bureau-flaws-in-same-sex-couple-data/

Cohn, D. (2011). *How accurate are counts of same-sex couples?* Retrieved from Pew Social and Demographic Trends website: http://www.pewsocialtrends.org/2011/08/25/how-accurate-are-counts-of-same-sex-couples/

Cohn, D., & Livingston, G. (2010). More women without children. Retrieved from Pew Research Center website: http://pewresearch.org/pubs/1642/more-women-without-children

Cohn, D., Livingston, G., Passel, J. S., & Wang, W. (2011). *Barely half of U.S. adults are married – a record low: New marriages down 5% from 2009 to 2010.* Retrieved from Pew Social and Demographic Trends Project website: www.pewsocialtrends.org/2011/12/14/barely-half-of-u-s-adults-are-married-a-record-low/

Coleman, E. (1985, Spring). Bisexual women in marriages. *Journal of Homosexuality, 11* (1–2), 87–99. Retrieved from http://www.ncbi.nlm.nih.gov/pubmed

Coontz, S. (2006). *Marriage, a history.* New York, NY: Penguin Group.

Copeland, P., and Hamer, D. (1994). *The science of desire: The search for the gay gene and the biology of behavior.* New York, NY: Simon & Schuster.

Davis, J. L. (2001, November 12). *What's so great about kissing?* Retrieved May 8, 2010, from MedicineNet.com website: http://www.medicinenet.com/script/main/art.asp?articlekey=51171

Dawkins, R. (1989). *The selfish gene.* New York, NY: Oxford University Press.

Dawkins, R. (2006). *The God delusion.* New York, NY: Houghton Mifflin Company.

Dawood, K., & Puts, D. A. (2006, June). The evolution of female orgasm: Adaption or byproduct? *Twin Research and Human Genetics 9,* (3), 467–472.

de Waal, F. (1995). Bonobo sex and society. *Scientific American, 272* (3), 82–89.

de Waal, F. (1995). *Our inner ape.* New York, NY: Penguin Group.

Denig, E. T. (1989). *Five Indian tribes of the upper Missouri.* Norman: University of Oklahoma Press.

Diamant, A.L., Lever, J., McGuigan, K., & Schuster, M.A. (1999, December 13/27). Lesbians' sexual history with men: Implications for taking a sexual history. *Archives of Internal Medicine, 159,* 2730–2736.

Diamond, J. (1993). *The third chimpanzee.* New York, NY: HarperCollins Publishers.

Diamond, J. (1999). *Guns, germs, and steel: The fates of human societies.* New York, NY: W. W. Norton & Company.

Durante, K. M., and Li, N. P. (2009, April 23). Oestradiol level and opportunistic mating in women. *Biology Letters, 5* (2), 179–182.

Economist. (2004, February 12). *I get a kick out of you.* Retrieved from oxytocin.org website: http://www.oxytocin.org/oxytoc/love-science.html

Elton, C. (2009, November 18). Female sexual dysfunction: Myth or malady? *Time.* Retrieved from http://www.time.com

Emlen, D. (1997, November). Alternative reproductive tactics and male dimorphism in the horned beetle Onthophagus acuminatus (Coleoptera: Scarabaeidae). *Behavioral Ecology and Sociobiology, 41* (5), 335–341.

Enserink, M. (2005, June). Let's Talk About Sex and Drugs. *Science, 308* (5728), 578.

Etcoff, N. (2000). *Survival of the prettiest: The science of beauty.* New York, NY: Anchor Books.

Fausto-Sterling, A. (1993, March/April). The five sexes: Why male and female are not enough. *The Sciences*, 20–24.

Fein, E. & Schneider, S. (2007). *All the rules: Time-tested secrets for capturing the heart of Mr. Right.* New York, NY: Hatchet Book Group USA.

Fertility sparks 'male rivalry'. (2006, April 25). *BBC News World Edition.* Retrieved from http://news.bbc.co.uk

Fielding, W. J. (1942). *Strange customs of courtship and marriage.* Philadelphia, PA: The Blakiston Company.

Finkel, E. J., Gable, S. L., Impett, E. A., & Strachman, A. (2008). Maintaining sexual desire in intimate relationships: The importance of approach goals. *Journal of Personality and Social Psychiatry, 94* (5), 808–823. Doi: 10.1037/0022-3514.94.5.808

Fisher, H. (1994). *Anatomy of love: A natural history of mating, marriage, and why we stray.* New York, NY: Random House Publishing Group.

Frank, P. W. (1981). A condition for sessile strategy. *The American Naturalist, 118,* 288–290.

Fry, R., Kochhar, R., & Taylor, P. (2011, July 26). *Wealth gaps widen to record highs between whites, blacks and hispanics.* Retrieved from Pew Research Center website: http://pewsocialtrends.org/2011/07/26/wealth-gaps-rise-to-record-highs-between-whites-blacks-hispanics/

Gagnon, J. H., Kolata, G., Laumann, E. O., & Michael, R. T. (1994). *Sex in America: A definitive survey.* New York, NY: Warner Books.

Gagnon, J. H., Laumann, E. O., Michael, R. T. & Michaels, S. (1994). *The social organization of sexuality: Sexual practices in the United States.* Chicago, IL: University of Chicago Press.

Gangestad, S. W., & Simpson, J. A. (2000). The evolution of human mating: Trade-offs and strategic pluralism. *Behavioral and Brain Sciences, 23,* 573–644.

Gangestad, S. W., Garver-Apgar, C. E., & Thornhill, R. (2005). Women's sexual interests across the ovulatory cycle depend on primary partner development instability. *Proceedings of the Royal Society B, 272*, 2023–2027. Doi 10.1098/rspb.2005.3112

Gender wars: A peace plan. (2009, October 1). *Psychology Today.* Retrieved from http://www.psychologytoday.com

George Sand. (2010, May 9). Retrieved May 26, 2010, from Wikipedia: http://en.wikipedia.org/wiki/George_Sand

Gilding, M. (2009). Paternity uncertainty and evolutionary psychology: How a seemingly capricious occurrence fails to follow laws of greater generality. *Sociology, 43* (1), 140–157. Doi: 10.1 177/0038038508099102

Gilding, M. (n.d.). *Using sex surveys to calculate the extent of paternal discrepancy.* Retrieved from The Austrialian Sociological Association website: http://www.tasa.org.au/conferences/conferencepapers07/papers/17.pdf

Gleick, J. (2011, May). Have meme, will travel. *Smithsonian, 43* (2), 88–94.

Goldstein, J. S. (2001). *War and gender: How gender shapes the war system and vice versa.* Cambridge, England. Cambridge University Press.

Goodstein, D. (1994, September 19). *The Big Crunch.* Paper presented at the National Conference on the Advancement of Research 48 Symposium, Portland, OR.

Gottman, J. M. (1995). *Why marriages succeed or fail.* New York, NY: Simon and Schuster.

Gottman, J. M., & Silver, N. (1999). *The seven principles for making marriage work.* New York, NY: Three Rivers Press.

Greenberg, D. (1990). *The construction of homosexuality.* Chicago, IL: University of Chicago Press.

Griffith, S. C., Owens, I. P., & Thuman, K. A. (2002). Extra pair paternity in birds: A review of interspecific variation and adaptive function. *Molecular Ecology, 11,* 2195–2212.

Guthrie, S. L. (2001). *Empiricism, naturalism, and theism.* Retrieved from http://www.sguthrie.net/empiricism.htm

Hamilton, B. E., Kirmeyer, S., Martin, J. A., Mathews, T. J., Menacker, F., Sutton, P. D., & Ventura, S. J. (2009, January 7). Births: Final data for 2006. *National Vital Statistics Reports, 57* (7), 1–13.

Harrell, S. (1997). *Human families.* Boulder, CO: Westview Press.

Harrison, J. R. (2003). *The nitrogen cycle: Of microbes and men.* Retrieved from VissionLearning website: http://www.visionlearning.com/library/module_viewer.php?mid=98

Haslam, N. (1997, October). Evidence that male sexual orientation is a matter of degree. *Journal of Personality and Social Psychology, 73* (4), 862–870. Abstract retrieved from http://www.ncbi.nlm.nih.gov/pubmed/

Hawley, J. S. and Narayanan, V. (Eds.). (2006). *The life of Hinduism.* Berkeley: University of California Press.

Hayden, T., and Potts, M. (2010). *Sex and war: How biology explains warfare and terrorism and offers a path to a safer world.* Dallas, TX: Benbella Books.

Heine, K. (2005, November 1). *A little perspective on marriage.* Retrieved from AZ Central website: http://www.azcentral.com/families/articles/1101marriageevolution01.html

Heterosexual-homosexual continuum. (2010, March 18). Retrieved March 19, 2010, from Wikipedia website: http://en.wikipedia.org/wiki/Heterosexual-homosexual_continuum

Heussner, K. M. (2010, July 8). Addicted to love? It's not you, it's your brain: Recovering from heartbreak is like kicking a drug addiction, study says. *ABC News*. Retrieved from http://www.abcnews.go.com

High hormone levels in women may lead to infidelity, study shows. (2009, January 30). *Science Daily*. Retrieved May 25, 2009, from http://www.sciencedaily.com/releases/2009/01/090127133113.htm

Hinde, R. A. (1999). *Why gods persist*. New York, NY: Routledge.

Hinsch, B. (1990). *Passions of the cut sleeve: The male homosexual tradition in China*. New York, NY: Reed Business Information, Inc.

History of male circumcision. (2010, September 30). Retrieved October 3, 2010, from Wikipedia: http://en.wikipedia.org/wiki/History_of_male_circumcision

Hitchens, C. & Hitchens, P. (2010, October 12). *Can civilization survive without God?* Debate hosted by Pew Forum on Religion and Public Life. Retrieved from website: http://pewresearch.org/pubs/1785/hitchens-brothers-debate-does-civilization-need-religion

Hite, S. (2004). *The Hite report: A nationwide study of female sexuality*. New York, NY: Seven Stories Press. (Original work published in 1976)

Homma, Y., Poon, C. S., Saewyc, E. M., & Skay, C. L. (2008). Stigma management? The links between enacted stigma and teen pregnancy trends among gay, lesbian, and bisexual students in British Columbia. *Canadian Journal of Human Sexuality, 17* (3), 123–139. Retrieved from http://www.ncbi.nlm.nih.gov

Homosexual behavior in animals. (2009, May 19). Retrieved Jan 15, 2012, from Wikipedia website: http://en.wikipedia.org/wiki/Homosexuality_in_animals

Hooper, J. (2010, September 17). Pope's visit: Benedict tells politicians that religion is being marginalized. *The Guardian*. Retrieved from http://www.guardian.co.uk

Horne, C. F. (1915). The *Code of Hammurabi: An Introduction*. Retrieved from Internet Ancient History Sourcebook website: http://www.fordham.edu/halsall/ancient/hamcode.asp#horne

Hrdy, S. B. (2000, April). The optimal number of fathers: Evolution, demography, and history in the shaping of female mate preferences. *Annals of the New York Academy of Sciences, 907,* 75–96.

Human-animal marriage. (2010, November 18). Retrieved November 17, 2010, from Wikipedia website: http://en.wikipedia.org/wiki/Human-animal_marriage

Italie, L. (2010, May 6). Study: Older, unmarried, educated moms on the rise. *Huffington Post*. Retrieved from http://www.huffingtonpost.com

Jahme, C. (2010, May 6). Penis size: An evolutionary perspective. *The Guardian*. Retrieved from http://www.guardian.co.uk

James, B. (1994, September 8). Overpopulation has a brief history. *The New York Times*. Retrieved from http://www.nytimes.com

Janssen, D. F. (2002, October). Aboriginal Australia. In *Growing Up Sexually. Volume I: World Reference Atlas*. Retrieved from Growing Up Sexually website: http://www2.hu-berlin.de/sexology/GESUND/ARCHIV/GUS/AUSTRALIAOLD.HTM

Jetha, C., and Ryan, C. (2010). *Sex at dawn: The prehistoric origins of modern sexuality*. New York, NY: HarperCollins Publishers.

Johns, C. H. (1910). Babylonian law — The Code of Hammurabi. In The Encyclopedia Britannica (11th ed.) New York City, NY: Encyclopaedia Britannica Inc.

Johnson, R. A. (1977). *SHE: Understanding feminine psychology.* New York, NY: Harper and Row.

Jones, S. L. (2002, June 22). Sexual script theory: An integrative exploration of the possibilities and limits of sexual self-definition. *Journal of Psychology and Theology, 30* (2), 120–131. Available from http://www.accessmylibrary.com

Joyce, K. (2009). *Quiverfull: Inside the Christian patriarchy movement.* Boston, MA: Beacon Press.

Kanazawa, S. (2008, April 20). Why do boys have cooties (but brothers don't) [Web log message]. Retrieved from PsychologyTodayBlogswebsite:http://www.psychology-today.com/blog/the-scientific-fundamentalist/200804/why-boys-have-cooties-brothers-don-t

Kelly, H. C. (1954, July 2). Trends in supply of scientists and engeneers in the United States. *Science, 120* (3105), 5a.

The Kinsey Institute. (n.d.). *Kinsey's heterosexual-homosexual rating scale.* Retrieved March 19, 2010, from http://www.kinseyinstitute.org/research/ak-hhscale.html

Kinsey Reports. (2010, February 23). Retrieved March 19, 2010, from Wikipedia website: http://en.wikipedia.org/wiki/Kinsey_Reports

Kinsey scale. (2010, March 15). Retrieved March 19, 2010, from Wikipedia website: http://en.wikipedia.org/wiki/Kinsey_scale

Kirkpatrick, R. C. (2000). The evolution of human homosexual behavior. *Current Anthropology, 41* (3), 385–413.

Klusmann, D. (n.d.). *Sperm competition and female procurement of male resources as explanations for a sex-specific time course in the sexual motivation of couples*. Retrieved from Universitätsklinikum Hamburg Eppendorf website: http://zpm.uke.uni-hamburg.de/WebPdf/SexMot2006.pdf

Klusmann, D. (n.d.). *Sexual motivation and the duration of partnership*. Retrieved from Universitätsklinikum Hamburg Eppendorf website: http://zpm.uke.uni-hamburg.de/Webpdf/sexmotiv.pdf

Knight, C. (2008). Early human kinship was matrilineal. In H. Callan (Ed.), *Early Human Kinship: From Sex to Social Reproduction* (pp. 61-82). Hoboken, NJ: John Wiley and Sons.

Koroda, K., Miyatake, T., Nomura, Y., & Okada, K. (2008). Fighting, dispersing, and sneaking: Body-size dependent mating tactics by male Librodor japonicus beetles. *Ecological Entamology, 33*, 269–275.

LaCroix, D. (n.d.). *Lights...camera...humor! A comedy secret for a professional presentation*. Retrieved from Fripp & Associates website: http://www.fripp.com/blog/lights-camera-humor-the-rule -of-three/

Leavitt, G. C. (2007). The incest taboo? A reconsideration of Westermarck. *Anthropological Theory, 7*, 393–491. Doi: 10.1177/1463499607083427

Lee, R. B. (1993). *The Dobe Ju/'hoansi* (2nd ed) (G. & L. Spindler, Eds.). Fort Worth, TX: Harcourt College Publishers.

Legal definition of adultery. (n.d.). Retrieved from The Free Online Law Dictionary website: http://legal-dictionary.thefreedictionary.com/adultery

Lewis, D. L. (2009). God's crucible: Islam and the making of Europe, 570–1215 (reprint ed.). New York, NY: W.W. Norton & Co.

Lloyd, E. A. (2005). *The case of the female orgasm: Bias in the science of evolution.* Cambridge, MA: Harvard University Press.

Mabe, M. (2003). The growth and number of journals. *Serials, 16* (2), 191–197.

Marriage. (2009, April 10). Retrieved April 10, 2009, from Wikipedia website: http://en.wikipedia.org/wiki/Marriage

Martin, J. (2005). *Miss Manners' guide to excruciatingly correct behavior. Freshly updated.* New York, NY: W. W. Norton & Company.

Moalem, S. (2010). *How sex works: Why we look, smell, taste, feel, and act the way we do.* New York, NY: Harper Perennial.

Monogamy. (2010, May 5). Retrieved May 9, 2010, from Wikipedia website: http://en.wikipedia.org/wiki/Monogamy

The Monogamy Puzzle. (2009, January 17). Retrieved from Life Without a Net: Morality, Meaning, and Happiness Without the Crutch of Religion website: http://hambydammit.wordpress.com/2009/01/17/the-monogamy-puzzle

Morris, D. (1967). *The naked ape.* New York, NY: McGraw-Hill.

Multiplemoms.com. (n.d.). *Twins with different fathers.* Retrieved from http://en.twinshome.gov.cn/ShowNews.asp?Big_Id=3&small_Id=3&NewsId=409

Mustanski, B. (2010, June 8). 25-year-long study finds children with lesbian parents may be better adjusted [Web log message]. Retrieved from Psychology Today website: http://www.psychologytoday.com/blog/the-sexual-continuum

National Science Foundation. (2010). *Growth rates for selected science and engeneering labor force measurements.* Retrieved from NSF website: http://www.nsf.gov/statistics/seind10/c3/c3s.htm

Nelson, R. (1994). *Babymaker: Fertility, fraud, and the fall of Doctor Cecil Jacobson.* New York, NY: Bantam Books.

Non-paternity event. (2009, March 13). Retrieved May 17, 2009, from Wikipedia website: http://en.wikipedia.org/wiki/Non-paternity_event

Office is the best bet for finding romance. (2007, May 18). Retrieved from News For Two website: http://news-for-two.cloudworth.com/local/6872.html

The origin of marriage [Web log message]. (2007, February 7). Retrieved April 10, 2009, from http://thearabobserver.blogspot.com/2007/02/origin-of-marriage.html

Oxytocin. (2010, May 6). Retrieved May 8, 2010, from Wikipedia website: http://en.wikipedia.org/wiki/Oxytocin

Pacey, A. A., & Suarez, S.S. (2006). Sperm transport in the female reproductive tract. *Human Reproduction Update, 12*(1), 23–37. doi: 10.1093/humupd/dmi047

Pair-bonding: A strength and a weakness. (2008, September 24). Retrieved from Reuniting: Healing with Sexual Relationships website: http://www.reuniting.info/science/pairbonding_strength_weakness

Paul, J. (n.d.). The Bisexual Identity. *Changing perspectives on sexuality: Contributions of Kinsey and anthroplolgists.* Retrieved from Connexions Library website: http://www.connexionx.org/CxLibrary/Doc/CX5017-BisexualIdentity.htm

Penn, N., & LaRose, L. (1998). *The code: Time-tested secrets for getting what you want from women – without marrying them.* New York, NY: Simon and Schuster.

Perrin, E.C. (2002, February). Technical report: Coparent of second-parent adoption by same-sex parents. *Pediatrics, 109* (2), 341–344.

Persaud, R. (1998, December 15). *Strategy in the human pair bond.* Retrieved from http://dotpeople.com/pairbond

Peterson, M. R. (1992). *At personal risk: Boundary violations in professional-client relationships.* New York, NY: W. W. Norton.

Pew Forum on Religion and Public Life. (2008, February). *U.S. religious landscape survey. Chapter 3: Religious Affiliation and Demographic Group.* Retrieved from Pew Forum on Religion and Public Life website: http://religions.pewforum.org/pdf/report-religious-landscape-study-chapter-3.pdf

Pew Forum on Religion and Public Life. (2010, September 28). U.S. religious knowledge survey. Executive summary retrieved from http://pewforum.org/U-S-Religious-Knowledge-Survey-Who-Knows-What-About-Religion.aspx

Pew Research Center. (2010). *The decline of marriage and rise of new families.* Retrieved from http://pewsocialtrends.org/2010/11/18/the-decline-of-marriage-and-rise-of-new-families

Pew Research Center. (2011). 91.*7%--minorities account for nearly all population growth.* Retrieved from http://pewresearch.org/databank/dailynumber/?NumberID=1225

Population control. (2010, February 10). Retrieved February 22, 2010, from Wikipedia website: http://en.wikipedia.org/wiki/Population_control

Quinlan, R. J. (2008, September/October). Human pair-bonds: Evolutionary functions, ecological variation and adaptive development. *Evolutionary Anthropology: Issues, News, and Reviews, 17* (5), 227–238.

Riddle, K. (2010, July 4). Kids first, marriage later — if ever. *National Public Radio.* Retrieved from http://www.npr.org

Robinson, M. (2009, October 29). The mysteries of pair bonding [Online exclusive]. *Psychology Today.* Retrieved from http://www.psychologytoday.com

Robinson, M. (2009, November 10). The mysteries of pair bonding (part two) [Online exclusive]. *Psychology Today*. Retrieved from http://www.psychologytoday.com

Rumor has it. (2012, January 14). Retrieved January 15, 2012, from Wikipedia website: http://en.wikipedia.org/wiki/Rumor_Has_It%E2%80%A6

Same-sex marriage. (2010, November 26). Retrieved November 27, 2010, from Wikipedia website: http://en.wikipedia.org/wiki/Same-sex_marriage

Sandfort, T. G. (2005, December). Sexual orientation and gender: Stereotypes and beyond. *Archives of Sexual Behavior, 34* (6), 595–611. Retrieved from http://www.ncbi.nlm.nih.gov/pubmed

Sexual Script. (2010, January 23). Retrieved January 29, 2010, from Wikipedia website: http://en.wikipedia.org/wiki/Sexual_script

Shepher, J. (1971). *Self-imposed incest avoidance and exogamy in second generation Kibbutz adults* (unpublished Ph.D. thesis). Rutgers University, New Brunswick, NJ.

Smil, V. (1997, July). Global Population and the Nitrogen Cycle. *Scientific American.* 76–81.

Solomon, R. C. (2006). *About love: Reinventing romance for our times.* Indianapolis, IN: Hackett Publishing Company.

Sparks, J. (1999). *Battle of the sexes: The natural history of sex.* New York, NY: TV Books, L.L.C.

Steiner, C. (1990). *Scripts people live: Transactional analysis of life scripts.* New York, NY: Grove Press.

Stewart, I. R. K., & Westneat, D. F. (2003, November). Extra-pair paternity in birds: Causes, correlates, and conflict. *Annual Review of Ecology, Evolution, and Systematics, 34,* 365–396. Abstract retrieved from annualreviews.org

Stookey, N. P. (1969). *The wedding song* [Musical composition].

Stuckey, J. (2005). Inanna and the "Sacred Marriage". *Matrifocus, 4* (2). Retrieved from http://www.matrifocus. com

Sultanoff, S. M. *What is humor?* (2010, May 19). Retrieved from Association for Applied and Therapeutic Humor website: http://www.aath.org/articles/art_sultanoff01.html

Sundaram, V. (2007, February 2). Indian feminists despair as film star marries a tree. *New America Media.* Retrieved from http://news.newamericamedia.org

Tattersall, I. (1998). *Becoming human: Evolution and human uniqueness.* New York, NY: Harcourt Brace & Company.

Taves, D. R. (2002, August). The intromission function of the foreskin. *Medical Hypotheses, 59* (2), 180–182. Retrieved from http://www.cirp.org/library

Till 2012 do us part? Mexico mulls 2-year marriage. (2011, September 29). Retrieved from Today website: http://today.msnbc.msn.com/id/44724855

Tonkinson, R. (1991). *The Mardu Aborigines: Living the dream in Australia's dessert* (2nd ed.) (G. & L. Spindler, Eds.). Belmont, CA: Wadsworth Group.

Types of marriages. (2010, October 18). Retrieved November 28, 2010, from Wikipedia website: http://en.wikipedia. org/wiki/Types_of_marriages

United Nations Demographic Yearbook: Focusing on Natality. (1999). *Table 13: Live Births by Legitimacy Status, and percent legitimate: 1990–1998.* Retrieved from website: http://unstats.un.org/unsd/demographic/products/dyb/dyb-nat.htm

U.S. Bureau of the Census. (1999). *Historical U.S. population growth by year 1900–1998.* Retrieved from National Population Growth website: http://www.npg.org/facts/us_historical_pops.htm

van den Berghe, P. L. (1990). *Human family systems: An evolutionary view*. Prospect Heights, IL: Waveland Press.

Varieties of monogamy. (n.d.). In *Worldlingo*. Retrieved January 27, 2011, from http://www.worldlingo.com/ma/enwiki/en/Varieties_of_monogamy

Vaughan, P. (2003). *The monogamy myth: A personal handbook for recovering from affairs*. (3rd ed.). New York, NY: Newmarket Press.

Vepachedu, S. (2000). *Tree marriages*. Retrieved from http://www.vepachedu.org

Wang, Z., & Young, L. J. (2004, October). The neurobiology of pair bonding. *Nature Neuroscience, 7* (10), 1048–1054. Doi: 10.1038/nn1327

Webster, P. (2002, August 4). Size did matter to Marie-Antoinette. *The Observer*. Retrieved from Guardian.co.uk/world/2002/aug/04/humanities.books

Weiner, J. (1987, March/April). When a snail leaves home. *The Sciences*. 6–10.

Westermarck, E. A. (1921). *The history of human marriage* (5th ed.). London, England: Macmillan.

Westermarck effect. Retrieved, from Psychology Wiki website: psychology.wikia.com/wiki/Westermarck_effect

Wiederman, M. (2005, October). The gendered nature of sexual scripts. *The Family Journal: Counseling and Therapy for Couples and Families, 13* (4), 496–502.

Wilson, P. (2002.) Analysis: Scientists, engineers and technical workers. In *Current statistics on scientists, engineers and technical workers: 2002 edition* [Publication]. Washington, DC: Department of Professional Employees, AFL-CIO.

Wolf, S. (1998). *Guerrilla dating tactics: Stratagies, tips, and secrets for finding romance*. New York, NY: Penguin Books.

Women prefer prestige over dominance in mates. (2008, December 23). *Science Daily*. Retrieved May 1, 2010, from http://www.sciencedaily.com/releases/2008/12/081217123825.htm

Women's Choice of Men Goes in Cycles. (1999, June 24). Retrieved from BBC News World Edition website: http://news.bbc.co.uk/2/hi/science/nature/376321.stm

World Population. (2010, March 3). Retrieved March 5, 2010, from Wikipedia website: httm://en.wikipedia.org/wiki/World_population

Wylie, K. (2007, December). Assessment and management of sexual problems in women. *Journal of the Royal Society of Medicine, 100*, 547–550.

Index

Homosexuality in sheep, 223
Human mating strategies,
    8-13, 44-52
Hunter-gatherer, 89, 96-99
Idiocracy, 167
Inactivity inertia, 76-77
Infidelity, 65, 96-99, 106-108
Inheritance, 102, 105-106
Intelligent Design, 173
Intelligentsia, 175
Irma Dunn, 155
Jacobson, Cecil, 53
Johnny Lee, 139
Kalahari Bushmen, 50, 98, 120
Katherine Hepburn, 15
Khomeini, Ayatollah, 112
King Louis XVI, 119
Kinsey, Alfred, 179, 196
Kneecap, 6
Kubler-Ross, Elizabeth, 31
Kung San, 98, 120
Laumann, Edward O., 15
Law of Unintended
    Consequences, 156, 161
Lee, Johnny, 139
Leo Tolstoy, 26
Leonardo da Vinci, 30
Lesbian motherhood
    genetics, 209
Lesbians and reproduction,
    208, 214
Libido, 128, 202-205
Libraries, 170-177
Limpet, 76-77
Lipstick lesbian, 205

Lloyd, Elizabeth, 129
Loneliness, fear of, 70, 78, 175
Long-term mate, 8, 44-53,
    140-142
Loss, fear of, 70, 78
Love, 23-34, 37-44
M. Scott Peck, 24
Mardu Aborigines, 96-97
Margaret Sanger, 155
Marginalization, of marriage,
    157-161
Marginalization, of religion,
    176-177
Marie Antoinette, 119
Marriage, and civil authorities,
    105
Marriage and religion, 105
Marriage, arranged, 90
Marriage, child, 90
Marriage, history of, 96-106
Marriage, history, pre-human,
    91-96
Marriage, Josephite, 90
Marriage, reasons for, 92-93
Marriage, same-sex, 89, 90,
    212-213
Marriage, variations on, 89-90
Mary Tyler Moore, 27, 164
Matrilinear (also Matrilocal),
    19-20, 100-101
Maugham, Somerset, 37,
    156, 231
Memes, 172
Meston, Cindy, 125
Monogamous species, 16

www.ingramcontent.com/pod-product-compliance
Lightning Source LLC
Chambersburg PA
CBHW060230050426
42448CB00009B/1381